Cross Stitch
Cuties

D&C
David and Charles

A DAVID & CHARLES BOOK
Copyright © David & Charles Limited 2007

David & Charles is an F+W Publications Inc. company
4700 East Galbraith Road
Cincinnati, OH 45236

First published in the UK in 2007

Charted designs copyright © Claire Crompton, Joan Elliott,
Jane Henderson, Ursula Michael, Joanne Sanderson and Lesley Teare 2007
Text and photographs copyright © David & Charles 2007

Claire Crompton, Joan Elliott, Jane Henderson, Ursula Michael,
Joanne Sanderson and Lesley Teare have asserted their right to
be identified as authors of this work in accordance with the
Copyright, Designs and Patents Act, 1988.

A catalogue record for this book is available from the British Library.

ISBN-13: 978-0-7153-2569-8 hardback
ISBN-10: 0-7153-2569-8 hardback

ISBN-13: 978-0-7153-2571-1 paperback
ISBN-10: 0-7153-2571-X paperback

Printed in
China by SNP Leefung Pte Ltd
for David & Charles
Brunel House   Newton Abbot   Devon

Executive Editor Cheryl Brown
Desk Editor Bethany Dymond
Project Editor and Chart Preparation Lin Clements
Head of Design Prudence Rogers
Senior Designer Tracey Woodward
Production Controller Ros Napper
Photography Kim Sayer and Michael Crocker

Visit our website at www.davidandcharles.co.uk

David & Charles books are available from all good bookshops;
alternatively you can contact our Orderline on 0870 9908222
or write to us at FREEPOST EX2 110, D&C Direct, Newton Abbot,
TQ12 4ZZ (no stamp required UK only); US customers call
800-289-0963 and Canadian customers call 800-840-5220.

Contents

Oh So Cute!

Discover a collection of utterly charming designs, all high on the cuteness scale and so filled with fun they are guaranteed to raise a smile.

There are quirky animals cavorting in four colourful seasonal settings, and also some larger than life creatures, showing us that big is not only beautiful but has a naughty sense of humour.

There is a chapter devoted to the sweetest of cats and the cuddliest of kittens, and also some whimsical dog designs that reflect everyday frustrations and challenges – perfect designs to stitch and make up as gifts for friends and family.

Some favourite toys appear too, including an adorable group of elephant, giraffe, duck and rabbit, in pretty pastel shades perfect for the nursery. There are teddies too, of course, with the sweetest couple celebrating the special event in a beautiful wedding sampler.

The innocence of childhood is captured with some darling little girls and boys in cameos you are sure to recognize, including an adorable ballerina and a keen sportsman. The fun of Christmas is celebrated with the merriest group of tubby Santas you've ever seen and the cutest of snow babies, all wrapped up for winter and ready to play.

All of these charming designs are shown made up in a variety of ways, including pictures, cards, bags, cushions, wedding accessories and Christmas decorations. There are also many 'More Cute Ideas' throughout the book, suggesting other ways to use the designs. Look out too for the Cute Sentiment sayings – short, sweet messages that you could use to personalize the designs further.

This original collection of versatile designs from six well-known cross stitch designers has something for everyone, whether you want a delightful picture to stitch or to create the smallest of greetings cards in next to no time.

Designed by
Jane Henderson

Animal Antics

These cute and quirky designs are such fun – who can resist smiling at the seasonal antics of these colourful characters? The Summer Daze design shows playful ducklings cooling off with a dip in the pond. Blooming Spring celebrates new life with a skipping lamb and Easter bunny, while Leaf Fall has fun bears kicking up autumn leaves and enjoying ripe fruit from the trees. Finally, there is Winter Wonders, where a speedy penguin determined to deliver his gifts on time reminds us of the excitement of Christmas and fun in the snow. Stitch these unusual and vibrant designs as an individual seasonal picture or as a set (see page 11), or simply pick out your favourite motif and add a sentiment to send a message to someone special – perfect for greetings cards.

Summer Daze Bag

Playful ducklings are frolicking in the pond in this gloriously sunny design. It has been attached to a handy drawstring bag made from fresh blue gingham fabric (see photo on previous page), but could also be mounted as a framed picture (see instructions on page 10).

Stitch count 100h x 100w
*
Design size 18.2 x 18.2cm (7⅛ x 7⅛in)

You will need

* White 14-count Aida 28 x 28cm (11 x 11in)
* Tapestry needle size 24
* DMC stranded cotton (floss) as listed in the chart key
* Iron-on interfacing: one piece 20 x 20cm (8 x 8in) and two pieces 40 x 30cm (16 x 12in) (if the bag fabric needs stiffening)
* Gingham fabric, two pieces 40 x 30cm (16 x 12in)
* Cord (or ribbon) for drawstring 3m (3¼yd)
* Satin ribbon 1m (1yd) long x 1.25cm (½in) wide
* Matching sewing thread

1 Prepare for work, referring to page 98 if necessary. Mark the centre of the fabric and centre of the chart. Mount your fabric in an embroidery frame if you wish.

2 Start stitching from the centre of the chart and fabric and work outwards over one block. Use two strands of stranded cotton (floss) for cross stitches and French knots and one strand for backstitches.

3 Once all stitching is complete, make the bag up as follows. Iron the interfacing on to the back of the embroidery and trim to about 19 x 19cm (7½ x 7½in). Iron the other two pieces of interfacing on to the two bag fabric pieces if necessary.

4 Pin the embroidery to the right side of one bag piece and tack (baste) ribbon all around the edge, mitring the corners. Machine stitch on either edge of the ribbon and on the corners.

5 On each piece of material fold over and sew down the top to form a channel 2.5cm (1in) deep, tucking the raw edge under neatly. Fold in the raw edges of the channel and stitch by hand. Place the two pieces of material right sides together and stitch down each side avoiding the channel.

6 Cut your cord (or ribbon) into two equal lengths and thread through the channel. Start each piece at one side, thread through both channels and come back out the same side. Pin the ends of the cords into the bottom seam at each side of the bag, ensuring the cord goes between the two right sides of material. Stitch across the bottom seam, taking care to go over the areas where the cords are attached a couple of times. Turn the bag right side out and press.

Winter Wonders Album

A starry sky, fresh snow, a Christmas tree and a penguin laden with presents remind us of the excitement of this seasonal time of year. Stitch the design as a cover for an album or perhaps as a little wall hanging for Christmas time.

1 Prepare for work, referring to page 98 if necessary. Mark the centre of the fabric and the centre of the chart on page 17. Mount your fabric in an embroidery frame if you wish.

2 Start stitching from the centre of the chart and the centre of the fabric and work outwards over one block of Aida. Use two strands of stranded cotton (floss) for cross stitches and for French knots and one strand for the backstitches.

3 Once all the stitching is complete, mount the embroidery on to your album as follows. Trim the embroidery eleven blocks out from the stitching all round. Carefully ease out a thread of Aida all the way around. Do this six more times to create a frayed edge.

4 Cut iron-on interfacing to cover the stitched design but not the frayed edge and fuse it to the back of the embroidery. Attach the embroidery to an album or book with double-sided tape or craft glue.

Cute Sentiment

Seasonal Pictures

Any of the four seasonal designs – Spring, Summer, Autumn and Winter – can be stitched individually as a picture, simply by following the instructions below. You could also work them together as a group, which will raise a smile throughout the year – see the layout opposite.

1 Prepare for work, referring to page 98 if necessary. Mark the centre of the fabric and centre of the chart (pages 14–17). Mount your fabric in an embroidery frame if you wish.

2 Start stitching from the centre of the chart and fabric and work outwards over one block. Use two strands of stranded cotton (floss) for cross stitches and French knots and one strand for backstitches.

3 Once all the stitching is complete, finish your picture by mounting and framing (see page 102).

Stitch count
(for each seasonal design)
100h x 100w
✳
Design size
18.2 x 18.2cm (7⅛ x 7⅛in)

More Cute Ideas. . .

Create a fun Easter card by stitching the rabbit and his basket of Easter eggs from the Blooming Spring design and add the message 'Happy Easter' using the sentiments charted on page 13.

This colourful design filled with fresh spring colours is bound to make you smile.

What a fun design this is! Any child would love this picture in their bedroom. Follow steps 1–3 opposite for stitching the design as an individual picture. Or why not work all four seasonal designs together as a group, as shown in the diagram below?

If you want to work all four designs together in a square layout like this you will need to work on a piece of 14-count Aida at least 61 x 61cm (24 x 24in) to allow for making up. Before you start to stitch, draw the plan out on graph paper and decide how much space you want between the designs, or whether you want to replace the border around each design with one border surrounding all four designs.

It might help you to photocopy all four charts and stick them together.

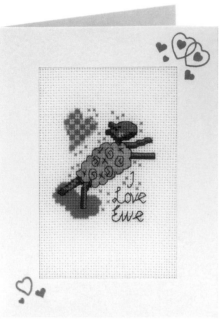

I Love Ewe
Valentine Card

Stitch count 43h x 39w
Design size 7.8 x 7cm (3 x 2¾in)

This sweet card is perfect for Valentine's Day or to send love at any time of year. Stitch it on white 14-count Aida following the chart opposite, using two strands of stranded cotton (floss) for cross stitches and French knots and one strand for backstitches. Mount your embroidery into a double-fold card as described on page 101. Add peel-off hearts or other embellishments of your choice.

Cool Yule
Christmas Card

Stitch count 70h x 46w
Design size 12.7 x 8.3cm (5 x 3¼in)

This fun card is given an extra festive touch by the addition of some peel-off stars. Change the greeting using the chart opposite. Stitch it on white 14-count Aida following the chart, using two strands of stranded cotton (floss) for cross stitches and French knots and one strand for backstitches. Mount your embroidery into a double-fold card (see page 101) and then add your embellishments.

More Cute Ideas...

The four seasonal designs have a wealth of detail so why not use them to create smaller projects? Stitch a quick Christmas card by working the decorated Christmas tree from Winter Wonders along with the words 'Happy Xmas'.

Use this sentiments chart to personalize the designs in this chapter or to add a sentiment to smaller projects of your own, changing the colours as desired

Cool Yule Christmas Card
DMC stranded cotton

Cross stitch				
307	415	963	• blanc	
318	957	996		
414	959	3078		

Backstitch
— 796
— 996

French knots
● 796

I Love Ewe
Valentine Card
DMC stranded cotton
Cross stitch

208	957
210	963
307	3078

Backstitch
— 150
— 801

French knots
● 801

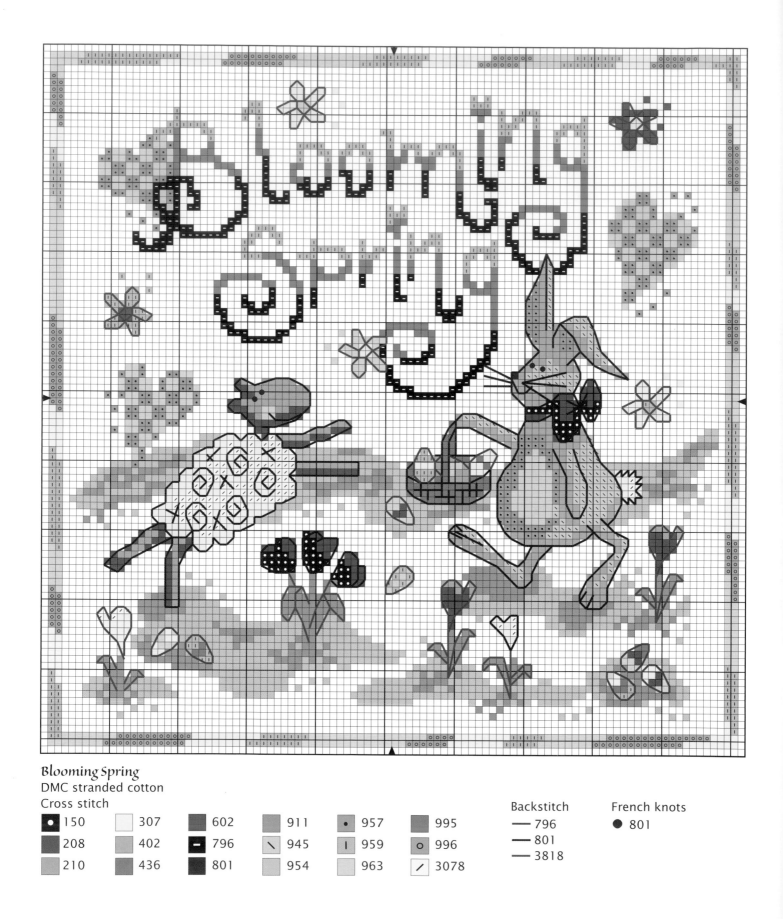

Blooming Spring
DMC stranded cotton
Cross stitch

150	307	602	911	• 957	995
208	402	▬ 796	\ 945	I 959	○ 996
210	436	801	954	963	/ 3078

Backstitch
— 796
— 801
— 3818

French knots
● 801

Summer Daze
DMC stranded cotton
Cross stitch

	307	▬	796		954	∕	3078	
	436		911		995		3341	
	606	▬	947	○	996	•	blanc	

Backstitch
— 796
— 3818

French knots
● 796

Leaf Fall
DMC stranded cotton
Cross stitch

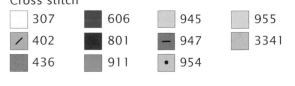

☐ 307	606	945	955
╱ 402	801	─ 947	3341
436	911	• 954	

Backstitch
— 436
— 801
— 911
— 947
— 3818

French knots
● 801

Winter Wonders

DMC stranded cotton

Cross stitch

▨ 208	▮ 318	▨ 436	▨ 954	▨ 963	╱ 3078		
▨ 210	▮ 414	▨ 602	╲ 957	▨ 995	• blanc		
▨ 307	▨ 415	▨ 911	V 959	○ 996			

Backstitch

— 307
— 796
— 996
— 3346

French knots

● 796

Designed by
Joanne Sanderson

Nursery Dreams

Who could resist this adorable group of nursery toys adorning a beautiful Afghan cot blanket? Stitched in baby-soft pastel colours, these favourite toys from childhood snuggled into fluffy white clouds are the perfect characters to shower love on your little one. As a special touch, the sweet blessing is surrounded by moon and stars worked in glow-in-the-dark thread. If you prefer, the central panel of the blanket could be stitched alone as a lovely picture for the nursery wall, while the small border motifs can be used in a variety of projects, such as a baby's bib, a welcome baby card and a keepsake album, all described on pages 21 and 22.

Nursery Dreams Blanket

This delightful cot blanket is sure to become a treasured possession. The stars and moon are stitched using white fluorescent thread to make them glow in the dark.

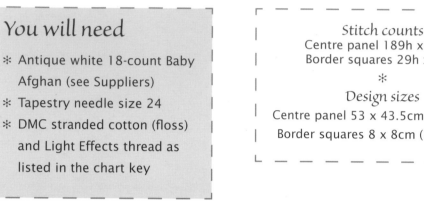

You will need

* Antique white 18-count Baby Afghan (see Suppliers)
* Tapestry needle size 24
* DMC stranded cotton (floss) and Light Effects thread as listed in the chart key

Stitch counts
Centre panel 189h x 154w
Border squares 29h x 29w

✱

Design sizes
Centre panel 53 x 43.5cm (21 x 17in)
Border squares 8 x 8cm (3¼ x 3¼in)

Afghan blanket layout showing positions of the various motifs

1 Prepare for work, referring to page 98 if necessary. Mark the centre of the central Afghan panel and start stitching from the centre of the chart on pages 24–27 working over two threads. Use three strands of stranded cotton for all full and three-quarter cross stitches and two strands for French knots. Use two strands for backstitch lettering and one strand for all other backstitches.

2 For the blanket border, stitch the six border squares (charts on page 28) in the centres of the Afghan border squares, repeating as necessary (see layout diagram, left). Note: it may be easier to place the motifs if each of the outer green border lines are stitched first.

3 Once stitching is complete, create a fringe by running a machine stitch 7cm (2¾in) from the outer raised threads on all four sides. Remove the threads up to the stitching line.

Bunny Bib

This sweet baby's bib is a quick-stitch project. It features a pink bunny but any of the small motifs from the Afghan blanket border could be used. The bibs are available in different colours and are suitable for a baby girl or boy.

> Stitch count 21h x 22w
> ✳
> Design size 3.8 x 3.8cm (1½ x 1½in)

You will need

* ✳ Baby's bib with 14-count cross stitch insert (see Suppliers)
* ✳ Tapestry needle size 26
* ✳ DMC stranded cotton (floss) as listed in the chart key

1 Find the centre of the cross stitch insert on the bib and start stitching here following the chart of your choice on page 28. The border around the motif has been omitted but you could include it if you wish. Note: you will not need all of the colours in the key.

2 Work over one block and use two strands of stranded cotton for cross stitch and one for backstitch. After the stitching is complete press the bib.

More Cute Ideas...

You could work all the border designs on squares of plastic canvas for a sweet mobile for a baby's room. Trim excess canvas from each motif and back with felt and then sew the motifs together with long lengths of pretty ribbon and hang from a decorative hanger.

Duckling Card

This charming card is the perfect welcome for a new baby. The design can be stitched for a boy or girl, with the colour of the card and ribbon changed to suit.

> Stitch count 49h x 41w ✷ Design size 9 x 7.5cm (3½ x 3in)

You will need

- ✷ White 14-count Aida 18 x 15cm (7 x 6in)
- ✷ Tapestry needle size 24
- ✷ DMC stranded cotton (floss) as listed in the chart key
- ✷ Ribbon bow to tone with embroidery
- ✷ Sheet of white card and pale blue card
- ✷ Rickrack braid or decorative trim
- ✷ Double-sided tape and craft glue

1 Prepare for work, referring to page 98 if necessary. Mark the centre of the fabric and centre of the chart on page 29. Start stitching from the centre of the chart and fabric and work over one block. Use two strands of stranded cotton (floss) for cross stitches and one for backstitches.

2 Once all stitching is complete, trim to eight rows beyond the design. Use craft glue to stick on the ribbon bow.

3 Make up the card as follows. Use double-sided adhesive tape to fix the embroidery on to a piece of coloured card 15 x 13.5cm (6 x 5½in). Glue the trim around the edges of the fabric. Fold a piece of white card 16 x 29cm (6¼ x 11½in) in half and stick the mounted design centrally on the front.

Teddy Album

A keepsake album for photographs and memorabilia is a must for any proud new parents and a sweet teddy is perfect to decorate the cover.

> Stitch count 56h x 45w
> ✷
> Design size 10.2 x 8.2cm (4 x 3¼in)

You will need

- ✷ White 14-count Aida 18 x 15cm (7 x 6in)
- ✷ Tapestry needle size 24
- ✷ DMC stranded cotton (floss) as listed in the chart key
- ✷ Photograph album (see Suppliers)
- ✷ Four small buttons
- ✷ Sheet of white card and deep yellow card
- ✷ Decorative cord or self-adhesive ribbon
- ✷ Double-sided tape and craft glue

1 Follow step 1 above to stitch the design. Once all stitching is complete, trim the embroidery to four rows beyond the design. Stitch a button in each corner of the border.

2 Complete the album as follows. Use double-sided tape to fix the embroidery to a piece of yellow card 15 x 13.5cm (6 x 5¼in). Fix decorative braid or self-adhesive ribbon around the edge of the fabric. Round the corners of the card with scissors and use double-sided tape to fix the mounted fabric on the front of the album.

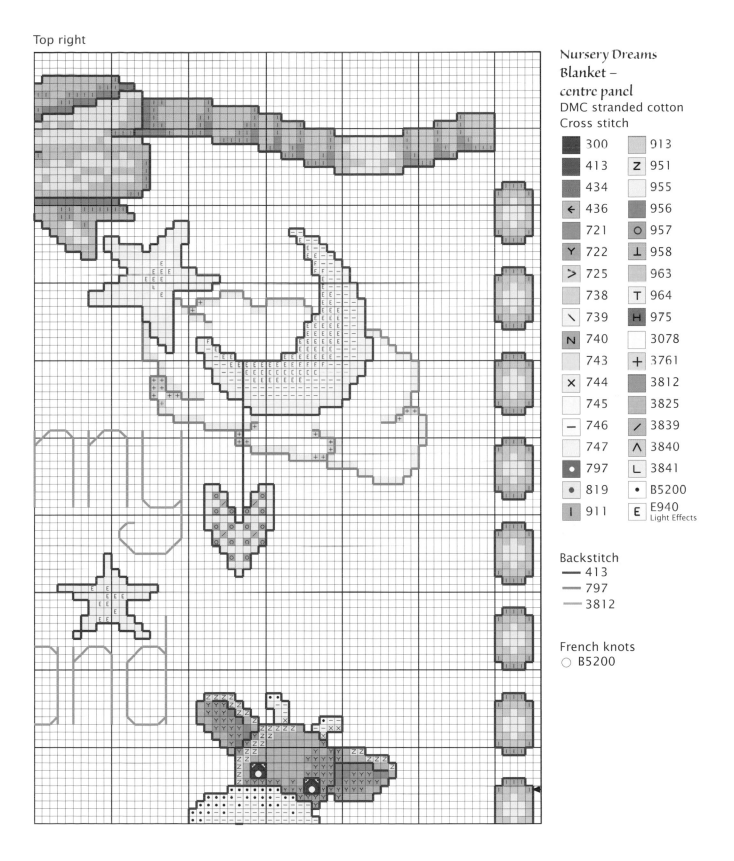

**Nursery Dreams
Blanket –
centre panel**
DMC stranded cotton
Cross stitch

	300		913
	413	Z	951
	434		955
←	436		956
	721	O	957
Y	722	⊥	958
>	725		963
	738	T	964
\	739	H	975
N	740		3078
	743	+	3761
×	744		3812
	745		3825
−	746	/	3839
	747	∧	3840
•	797	L	3841
•	819	•	B5200
I	911	E	E940 Light Effects

Backstitch
—— 413
—— 797
—— 3812

French knots
○ B5200

Bottom left

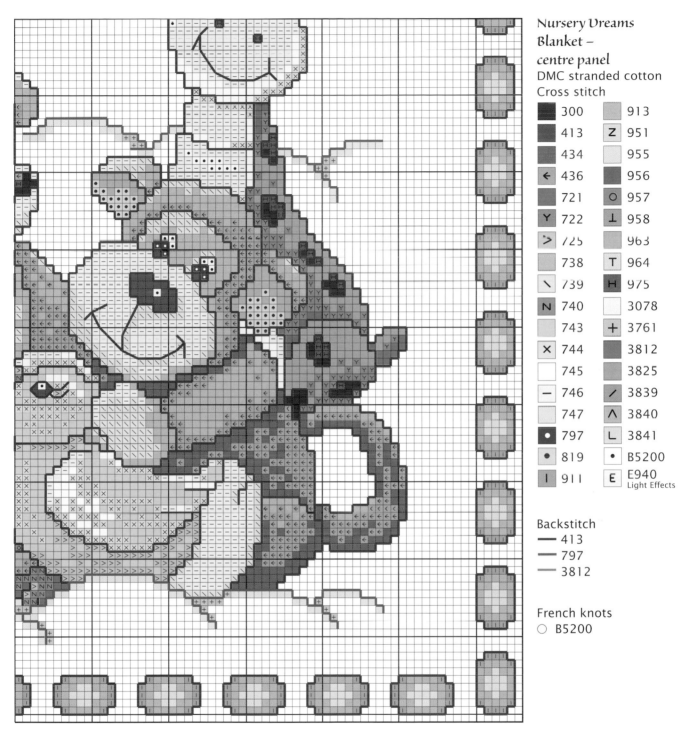

Nursery Dreams Blanket – centre panel

DMC stranded cotton

Cross stitch

■	300		913
■	413	Z	951
	434		955
←	436		956
	721	O	957
Y	722	⊥	958
>	725		963
	738	T	964
\	739	H	975
N	740		3078
	743	+	3761
×	744		3812
	745		3825
−	746	/	3839
	747	∧	3840
⊙	797	L	3841
•	819	•	B5200
I	911	E	E940 Light Effects

Backstitch
— 413
— 797
— 3812

French knots
○ B5200

Bottom right

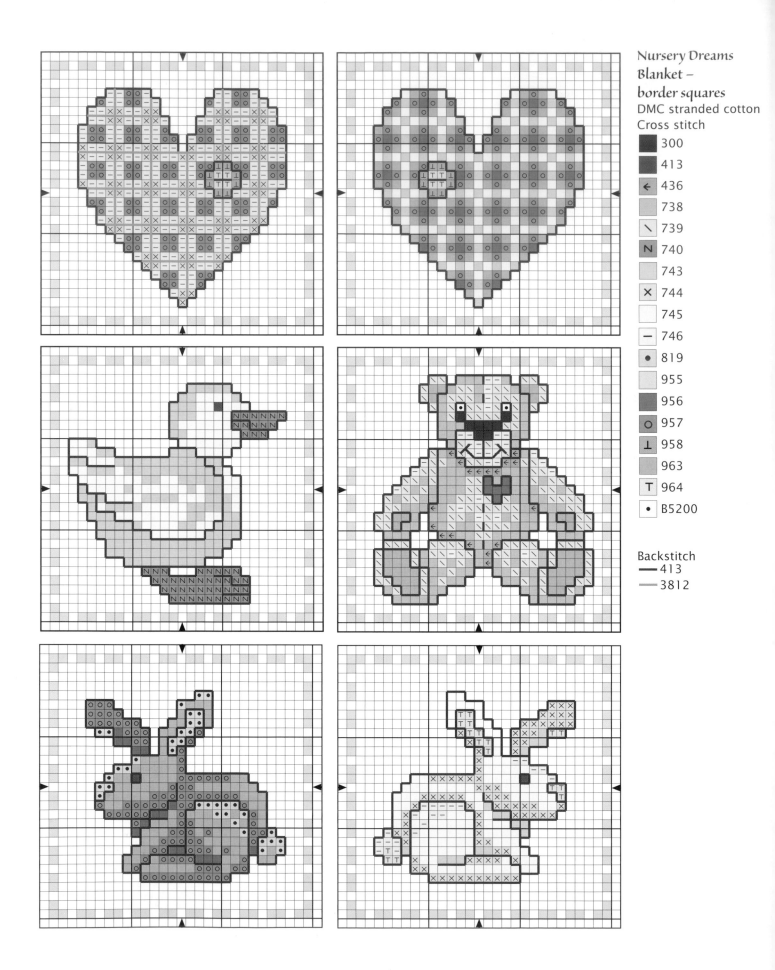

Nursery Dreams
Blanket –
border squares
DMC stranded cotton
Cross stitch

■	300
■	413
←	436
	738
\	739
N	740
	743
×	744
	745
−	746
•	819
	955
	956
O	957
⊥	958
	963
T	964
•	B5200

Backstitch
—— 413
—— 3812

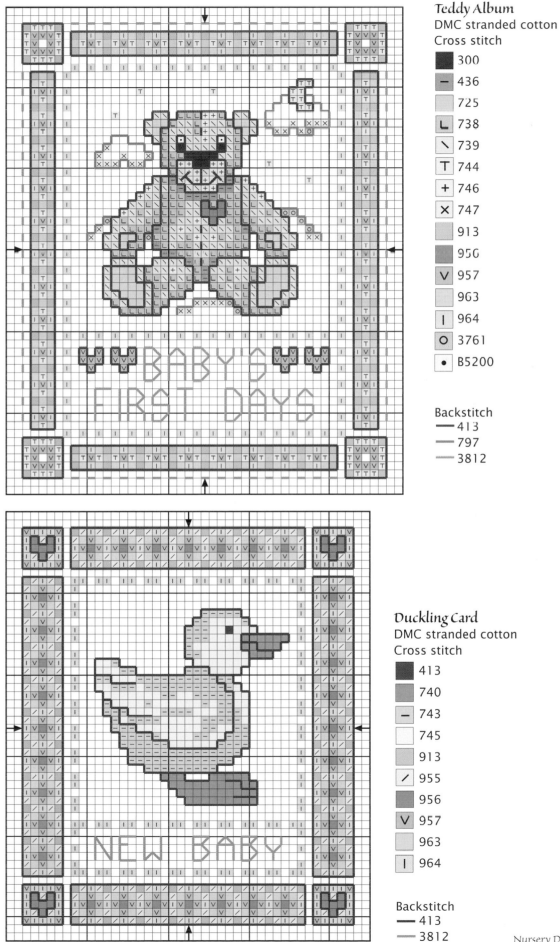

Teddy Album
DMC stranded cotton
Cross stitch

■	300
−	436
	725
L	738
\	739
T	744
+	746
×	747
	913
	956
V	957
	963
I	964
O	3761
•	B5200

Backstitch
—— 413
—— 797
—— 3812

Duckling Card
DMC stranded cotton
Cross stitch

■	413
	740
−	743
	745
	913
/	955
	956
V	957
	963
I	964

Backstitch
—— 413
—— 3812

Designed by
Claire Crompton

Big is Beautiful

Larger than life and rating high on cuteness factor, the amusing characters in this chapter will make fun additions to any home. For the bathroom, create a picture of a dainty hippo all fresh from the bath and determined to ignore the scales and have fun. There is also a leggy ostrich in a mass of fluffy feathers – perfect to stitch and make up into a useful laundry bag for your delicate little items.

For the kitchen, stitch a cuddly, tubby bear, who quite rightly points out that 'round is a shape', and then decorate a recipe book cover with a naughty gorilla who thinks 'eat 5-a-day' refers to chocolate cakes. These designs would also make a great set of framed pictures for a child or teenager's room.

Ostrich Bag

A drawstring bag decorated with a fun ostrich will be the perfect laundry bag for your delicate bits and pieces (see photograph on the previous page). The bag can be made in any size you wish.

1 Prepare for work, referring to page 98 if necessary. Mark the centre of the fabric and the centre of the chart on page 36. Mount your fabric in an embroidery frame if you wish.

2 Start stitching from the centre of the chart and fabric. Working over one block, use two strands of stranded cotton (floss) for all full and three-quarter cross stitches. Work DMC 3371 backstitches with one strand and use two strands for the backstitch writing in 552.

3 Once all stitching is complete, make up into a drawstring bag as follows. Fuse the iron-on interfacing to the wrong side of the embroidery according to the manufacturer's instructions. Trim the embroidery about 2cm (¾in) beyond the widest part of the design. Turn under the raw edges 1cm (⅜in) and tack (baste) down. Place the patch on to one of the bag pieces 6.3cm (2½in) up from the bottom edge and centralize. Sew the patch on to the bag piece using matching cotton and small running stitches (use the Aida squares as a guide). Remove tacking (basting) thread.

4 Place the two pieces of bag fabric right sides together. Leaving 14cm (5½in) open at the top on both sides, stitch a 1.25cm (½in) seam along the bottom and up both sides. Trim the bottom corners diagonally and press seams open. Turn the bag to the right side. Finish the raw edge by turning it over 6mm (¼in), then press and stitch close to the edge. Turn the top of the bag to the inside about 6.5cm (2½in) to make a hem and channel for the drawstring and press. Stitch a line 5.5cm (2¼in) from the folded edge and another line 4.5cm (1¾in) from the folded edge to create a channel.

5 Thread two 81cm (32in) lengths of ribbon through the casing in opposite directions for a drawstring. Knot together each pair of ribbon ends and trim the ends into points to prevent fraying. To finish, pull each end to gather.

Hippo Picture

Big certainly is beautiful! Stitching this fun picture for your bathroom will start each day with a smile (see photo on page 31).

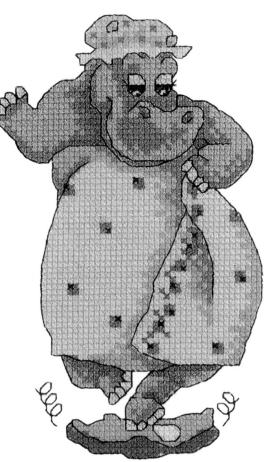

Stitch count
93h x 73w

✳

Design size
17 x 13.3cm (6¾ x 5¼in)

You will need

✳ Pink 14-count Aida
  28 x 23cm (11 x 9in)
✳ Tapestry needle size 24–26
✳ DMC stranded cotton (floss)
  as listed in the chart key

1 Prepare for work, referring to page 98 if necessary. Mark the centre of the fabric and chart on page 37. Mount your fabric in an embroidery frame if you wish.

2 Start stitching from the centre of the chart and fabric. Working over one block, use two strands of stranded cotton (floss) for all full and three-quarter cross stitches. Work DMC 3371 backstitches with one strand and use two strands for the backstitch writing in 553.

3 Once all stitching is complete, make up into a framed picture following the advice on page 102.

Bear Picture

Stitch this great design as a picture for your kitchen (see photo on page 35) or perhaps as a companion to the hippo design. Work on a 28 x 23cm (11 x 9in) piece of 14-count sage green Aida and follow the chart on page 38, using two strands of stranded cotton (floss) for full and three-quarter cross stitches. Work DMC 3371 backstitches with one strand and use two strands for the backstitch writing in 310. Use two strands for long stitch in 760. Once all the stitching is complete, make up into a framed picture (see page 102).

Stitch count
98h x 73w

✳

Design size
18 x 13.3cm (7 x 5¼in)

Gorilla Book Cover

This naughty gorilla is the perfect chap to decorate the front of a recipe book, especially if you use it to hold your favourite 'wicked' recipes.

You will need

* Lemon 14-count Aida
  23 x 23cm (9 x 9in)
* Tapestry needle size 24–26
* DMC stranded cotton (floss)
  as listed in the chart key
* Fabric to cover book
* Medium-weight iron-on
  interfacing same size as Aida
* Hardback notebook, at least
  20 x 20cm (8 x 8in)

1 Prepare for work, referring to page 98 if necessary. Mark the centre of the fabric and the centre of the chart on page 39. Mount your fabric in an embroidery frame if you wish.

2 Start stitching from the centre of the chart and fabric. Working over one block, use two strands of stranded cotton (floss) for full and three-quarter cross stitches and one strand for backstitches.

3 Once all stitching is complete, make up into a book cover as follows. Fuse the iron-on interfacing to the wrong side of the finished embroidery according to the manufacturer's instructions. Trim the embroidery 2cm (¾in) beyond the widest measurements of the design shape. Turn under the raw edges 1cm (⅜in) and tack (baste) down.

4 With the book closed, measure from the front edge around the book spine to the opposite edge (call this A). Measure the length of the book from top to bottom edge (call this B). Add 15cm (6in) to measurement A and 3.5cm (1½in) to B and cut out two pieces of fabric using these measurements.

5 Make the book cover by placing the two fabric pieces right sides together. Leaving one side edge open, stitch a 1.25cm (½in) seam along the bottom, top and one side. Turn to the right side and press the seams flat. Turn the raw edges in 1.25cm (½in) and stitch the remaining side edge closed. To make flaps to slot the book covers into, fold each side edge in 6cm (2¼in) and pin along the top and bottom edges. Machine or hand sew through all thicknesses.

6 Put the cover on to the book by pushing the book covers into the flaps. Pin the embroidery on the front. Remove the book and sew the patch on the cover using matching thread and small running stitches. To finish, fit the cover back on the book.

Ostrich Bag
DMC stranded cotton
Cross stitch

310	415	761
318	452	762
413	453	801

3371
ecru
blanc

Backstitch
— 552 (2 stands)
— 3371

Hippo Picture
DMC stranded cotton
Cross stitch

153	415	550	· 762	963	I 3822
− 318	469	✓ 553	801	↘ 3716	ecru
414	471	644	O 962	3820	

Backstitch
— 553 (2 strands)
— 3371

Bear Picture
DMC stranded cotton
Cross stitch

319	437	○ 761	• blanc
320	▪ 677	841	
433	╲ 739	▮ 898	
╱ 435	760	3371	

Backstitch
— 310
(2 strands)
— 3371

Long stitch
— 760
(2 strands)

French knots
● 310

Gorilla Book Cover

DMC stranded cotton

Cross stitch

■ 349	■ 839	3822
469	\ 840	3864
/ 801	▌ 3031	• 3866

Backstitch

— 3371

Cute Sentiment

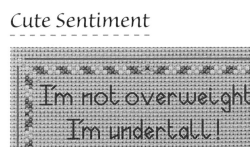

I'm not overweight, I'm under tall!

Designed by
Lesley Teare

It's a Cat's World

Time spent with cats is never wasted, whether it's watching their antics
as they play or stroking their silky fur as they snooze on your lap.
Certainly cats, and especially kittens, must rate near the top of the
cuteness scale and this chapter is filled with adorable designs made
up in pretty ways. All of the designs can be stitched and then framed
as attractive pictures but the cats and kittens are all so sweet you are
sure to be tempted to display them in other ways, such as the cushion
shown opposite or the nightdress case on page 45.

Dotty Kittens Cushion

This delightful design features two irresistible kittens at play. It has been made up into a cushion (shown on the previous page) but would also make a lovely framed picture.

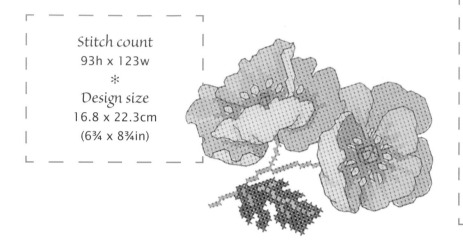

You will need

* White 14-count Aida 23 x 31cm (9 x 12in)
* Tapestry needle size 24
* DMC stranded cotton (floss) as listed in the chart key
* Lightweight iron-on interfacing 0.25m (¼yd)
* Fabric for cushion 0.5m (½yd)
* Narrow braid in a contrasting colour 1.25m (1¼yd)
* One decorative button
* Matching sewing thread
* Cushion pad

1 Prepare for work referring to page 98 if necessary. Mark the centre of the fabric and centre of the chart on pages 46–47. Mount your fabric in an embroidery frame if you wish.

2 Begin stitching from the centre of the fabric and chart and work outwards over one block. Work the full and three-quarter cross stitches using two strands of stranded cotton (floss). Work French knots with two strands of thread wound twice around the needle. Work backstitches with one strand.

3 Cut a piece of iron-on interfacing and fuse it to the back of the embroidery and then trim the embroidery to the size required.

4 Cut two pieces of cushion fabric 1.25cm (½in) larger than the cushion pad. Centre the stitched design on one piece of fabric and slipstitch in place all around the edge. Sew decorative cord all around the Aida and add a button where the raw ends meet.

5 Place the two cushion pieces right sides together and pin. Use matching sewing thread to stitch a 1.25cm (½in) seam all round, leaving an opening at the bottom for turning through. Turn through to the right side, insert the cushion pad and slipstitch the opening.

More Cute Ideas...

If time is short work just the left-hand kitten and poppy from the cushion design and use the embroidery to decorate a photo album.

Flowerpot Tabby Picture

This adorable tabby cat makes a perfect picture (shown on page 41) but you could also attach the design to the front of a notebook.

> Stitch count 95h x 70w
> *
> Design size 17.2 x 12.7cm (6¾ x 5in)

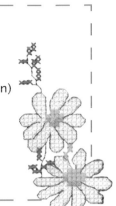

You will need

* ❋ Pale blue 14-count Zweigart Aida (code 5130) 25.5 x 23cm (10 x 9in)
* ❋ Tapestry needle size 24
* ❋ DMC stranded cotton (floss) as listed in the chart key
* ❋ Suitable picture frame

1 Prepare for work referring to page 98 if necessary. Mark the centre of the fabric and centre of the chart on page 48. Mount your fabric in an embroidery frame if you wish.

2 Begin stitching from the centre of the fabric and chart and work outwards over one block. Work full and three-quarter cross stitches using two strands of stranded cotton (floss). Work backstitches with one strand.

3 Once all the stitching is complete, finish your picture by mounting in a suitable frame (see page 102 for advice).

Snoozy Kitten Picture

The sweetest of kittens fast asleep on a cosy slipper makes a beautiful little picture (shown on page 45). Metallic thread and gold beads add a special touch.

> Stitch count 70h x 98w
> *
> Design size 12.7 x 18cm (5 x 7in)

You will need

* ❋ Ecru 14-count Aida 23 x 25.5cm (9 x 10in)
* ❋ Tapestry needle size 24 and a beading needle
* ❋ DMC stranded cotton (floss) as listed in the chart key
* ❋ Kreinik #4 Very Fine Braid, gold 002
* ❋ Mill Hill Petite glass beads, 40557 gold
* ❋ Suitable picture frame

1 Stitch the design following steps 1 and 2 above, using the chart on page 49. Attach the beads using a beading needle and matching thread (see page 100).

2 Once all stitching is complete, frame your picture (see page 102 for advice).

Cute Sentiment

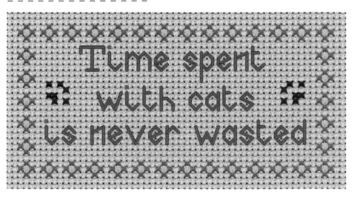

Cosy Cat Nightdress Case

Cats can get comfortable anywhere but especially perched on top of soft furnishings. This pretty design has been made up into a nightdress case but it could also be framed as a picture or be made into a cushion (see photograph opposite).

Stitch count 89h x 148w
*
Design size 16 x 27cm (6½ x 10½in)

You will need

* Pink 14-count Zweigart Aida (code 4430) 28 x 38cm (11 x 15in)
* Tapestry needle size 24
* DMC stranded cotton (floss) as listed in the chart key
* Zweigart white linen fabric for case 0.5m (½yd)
* Lightweight iron-on interfacing 0.25m (¼yd)
* Narrow cord 3m (3¼yd)
* One decorative button
* One silk tassel
* Matching sewing thread

1 Prepare for work, referring to page 98. Mark the centre of the fabric and the centre of the chart on pages 50–51. Mount fabric in an embroidery frame if you wish.

2 Begin stitching from the centre of the fabric and chart and work outwards over one block. Work the full and three-quarter stitches using two strands of stranded cotton (floss) and one strand for backstitches.

3 Once all the stitching is complete make up as a nightdress case as follows. Cut three pieces of linen 43 x 33cm (17 x 13in). Trim the embroidery to the size required and sew it to the front of one of the linen pieces. Starting and finishing at the centre bottom, slipstitch the cord around the design. Attach a decorative button where cord ends meet.

4 On the other two pieces of fabric make a fold of 10cm (4in) on the right, shorter sides of each. Neaten the edges of the folded pieces if necessary by oversewing. Place the right sides of these on top of each other to make an opening and then place both pieces on top of the front piece of fabric, right sides together (this is an Oxford-type case). Tack (baste) together and then machine sew with matching sewing thread 1.25cm (½in) from the edges. Mitre the corners and turn the case right side out.

5 Add the rest of the cord round the outer edge, starting and finishing at the centre bottom. Add the tassel where the cord finishes to neaten the ends.

More Cute Ideas...

The sleeping kitten design would be ideal made up as a sign to hang on the nursery door when a baby is napping. Back the finished embroidery with iron-on interfacing and then fold it over a piece of stiff card and stick in place on the back with double-sided tape. Add a hanger of narrow ribbon and glue felt over the back to neaten.

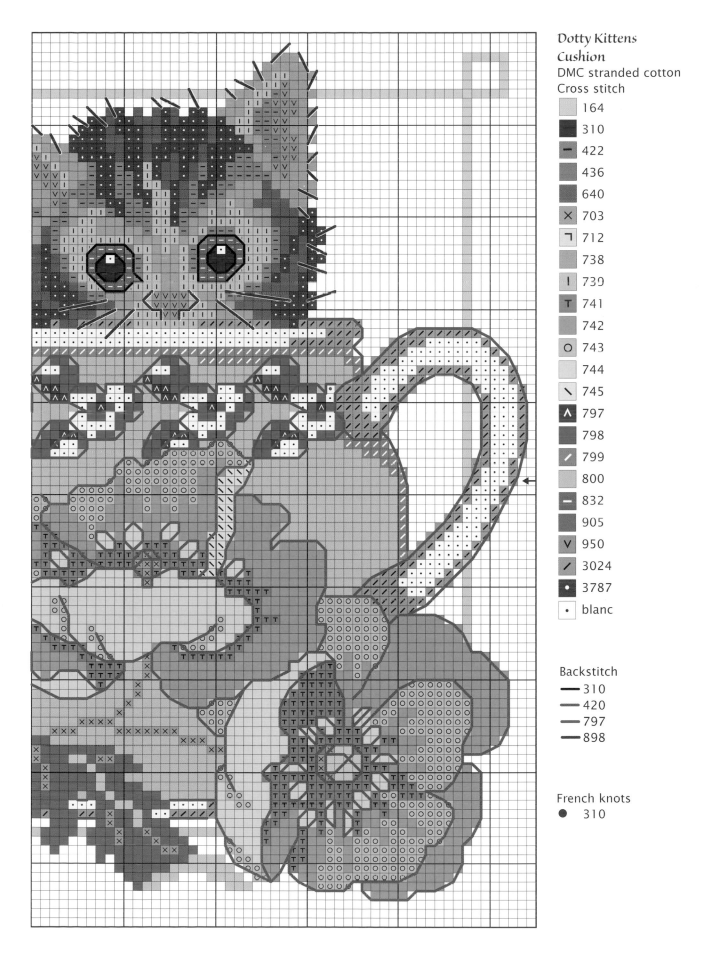

Dotty Kittens
Cushion
DMC stranded cotton
Cross stitch

	164
	310
−	422
	436
	640
×	703
⌐	712
	738
I	739
T	741
	742
O	743
	744
\	745
Λ	797
	798
/	799
	800
−	832
	905
V	950
/	3024
•	3787
·	blanc

Backstitch
— 310
— 420
— 797
— 898

French knots
● 310

Flowerpot Tabby
Picture
DMC stranded cotton
Cross stitch

Symbol	Color
╱	164
■	310
╲	420
	422
	703
∧	738
╲	739
T	741
	742
O	743
	744
×	745
+	832
V	840
−	841
•	898
	904
I	905
O	918
L	921
▲	950
+	3033
I	3064
Z	3779
U	3782
−	3823
	3862
•	blanc

Backstitch
—— 310
—— 898
—— 3862
⇀ blanc

Snoozy Kitten
Picture

DMC stranded cotton
Cross stitch

■	335
▨	677
▨	926
L	927
▨	928
▨	3046
O	3326
▨	3347
T	3756
▨	3779
▨	3835
▨	3836
L	3859
╲	3865
•	B5200

Backstitch
— 926
— 3859
— B5200
— Kreinik #4 braid
  (002 gold) (1 strand)

Mill Hill beads
◉ 40557 gold

49

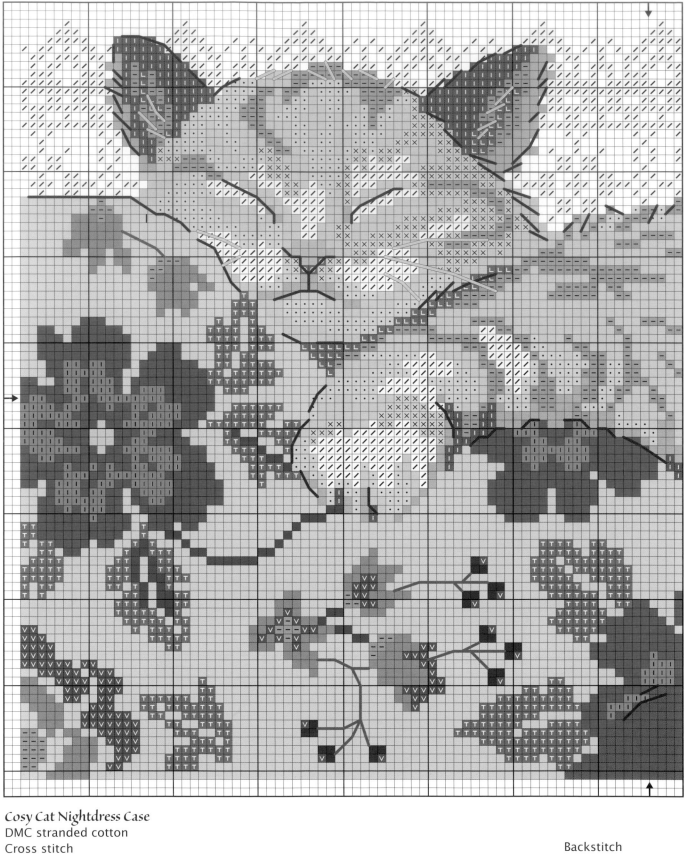

Cosy Cat Nightdress Case
DMC stranded cotton
Cross stitch

									Backstitch
■ 167	I 642	L 3045	■ 3346	■ 3834	O 3859	• ecru		— 611
■ 335	677	– 3046	T 3347	V 3835	✕ 3865			— 3345
613	772	I 3326	3779	3836	╱ B5200			═ ecru

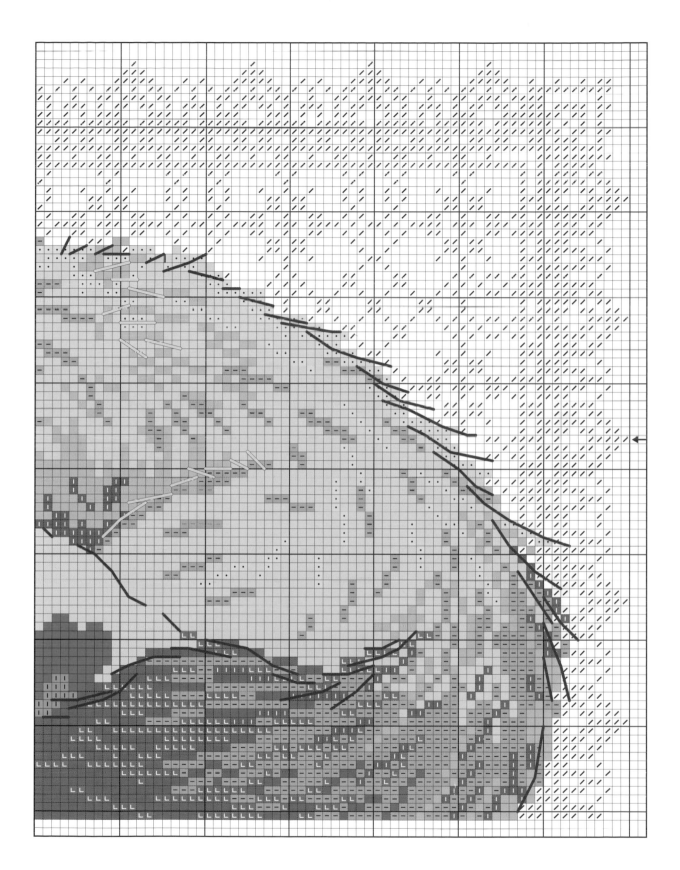

Designed by

Joan Elliott

Wedded Teddies

Come celebrate a joyous wedding day with a charming pair of teddy bears, an ever-endearing symbol of love and affection. Set on a field of hearts and flowers these two will surely live happily ever after. Use the included alphabet to personalize the wedding sampler with the names of your favourite couple. All the necessary accessories are also featured: a sweet ring pillow edged in lace, an adorable bridesmaid's bag matching the colours of the wedding party and a card bearing the word 'love' to complete the ensemble.

Wedded Teddies Sampler

Stitch count
151h x 108w
✳
Design size
27.5 x 19.5cm (10¾ x 7¾in)

You will need

✳ White 14-count Aida
40.5 x 33cm (16 x 13in)

✳ Tapestry needle size 24

✳ DMC stranded cotton (floss)
as listed in chart key

✳ Kreinik blending filament
#032 pearl

✳ Picture frame to fit
embroidery

This lovely sampler with its charming teddy bear couple is sure to bring pleasurable memories to the bride and groom. It is given an extra special touch by the addition of gleaming blending filament.

1 Prepare for work, referring to page 98 if necessary. Mark the centre of the fabric and centre of the chart on pages 58–59. Mount your fabric in an embroidery frame if you wish.

2 Start stitching from the centre of the chart and fabric. Use two strands of stranded cotton (floss) for all full and three-quarter cross stitches. Using two strands of Kreinik blending filament, overstitch with half cross stitch all DMC 762, 415, and white cross stitches in the veil and dress of the bride and the tie of the groom. Work French knots using two strands wound once around the needle and work backstitches using one strand. Use the alphabet on page 61 to stitch the names and date. Plan the letters on graph paper first to ensure they fit the space.

3 Once all the stitching is complete, finish your picture by mounting and framing (see page 102).

Stitch count
35h x 53w
✳
Design size
6.5 x 9.5cm (2½ x 3¾in)

Wedding Card

This simple card is quick to stitch but says it all. Stitch it on white 14-count Aida following the chart on page 57, using two strands of stranded cotton (floss) for cross stitches and French knots and one strand for backstitches. Mount your embroidery into a double-fold card as described on page 101. Add some satin ribbon and a rose or other embellishments of your choice.

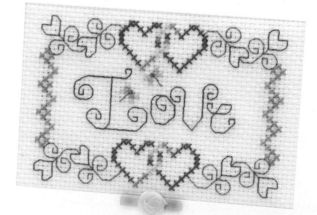

Ring Pillow

This gorgeous pillow edged with lace and pearls will display the wedding rings beautifully. You could also stitch just the central motif and names for a charming keepsake picture.

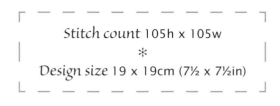

Stitch count 105h x 105w

✽

Design size 19 x 19cm (7½ x 7½in)

1 Prepare for work, referring to page 98 if necessary. Mark the centre of the fabric and chart on page 60. Mount your fabric in an embroidery frame if you wish.

2 Start stitching from the centre of the chart and fabric. Use two strands of stranded cotton (floss) for all full and three-quarter cross stitches. Work French knots using two strands wound once around the needle and work backstitches using one strand. Change the names and dates using the alphabet on page 61.

3 Once all stitching is complete, make up into a pillow as follows. Tack (baste) the thin ribbon to the centre of the embroidered bow. Trim the embroidery leaving twelve rows beyond the edge all around. Cut the interfacing to the same size as the trimmed embroidery and fuse to the wrong side following the manufacturer's instructions. Cut the backing fabric to the same size and pin in place, right sides facing. Using matching thread, stitch a 1.25cm (½in) seam all around, leaving a gap at the bottom. Turn through to the right side, stuff with polyester filling and slipstitch the gap.

4 Attach the decorative lace by slipstitching along the finished edge of the pillow, starting and ending at centre bottom. Carefully glue a strand of decorative pearls along the edge of the lace. Attach the rings to the pillow by tying the narrow ribbon in a pretty bow.

You will need

* White 14-count Aida 31.5 x 31.5cm (12½ x 12½in)
* Tapestry needle number 24
* DMC stranded cotton (floss) as listed in chart key
* 0.5m (½yd) thin ribbon to tone with embroidery
* 0.25m (¼yd) white satin fabric for backing
* 1.5m (1½yd) decorative lace
* 1.5m (1½yd) pearl trim
* Lightweight iron-on interfacing
* Polyester filling
* Permanent fabric glue

Bridesmaid's Bag

This sweet bag would be the perfect keepsake to thank a bridesmaid for her part in the wedding ceremony, perhaps filled with a sweet treat or little gift.

Stitch count 58h x 59w ✱ Design size 10.5 x 10.7cm (4⅛ x 4¼in)

1 Prepare for work, referring to page 98 if necessary. Mark the centre of the fabric and chart, opposite. Stitch the design following step 2 of the sampler on page 54.

2 Once all stitching is complete, make up into a drawstring bag as follows. Cut a piece of iron-on interfacing 2.5cm (1in) larger all around than the finished embroidery and fuse to the wrong side according to the manufacturer's instructions. Trim the embroidery 6mm (¼in) beyond the finished shape. Cut two pieces of interfacing 19 x 18cm (7½ x 7in) (or the size of your fabric pieces), align with the bottom edges of the two pieces of bag fabric, wrong sides facing and fuse together.

3 Make the bag by placing the two fabric pieces right sides together. Leaving 14cm (5½in) open at the top on both sides and using matching sewing thread, stitch a 1.25cm (½in) seam along the bottom and up both sides. Trim the bottom corners diagonally and press seams open. Turn to the right side. Turn the raw edge over 6mm (¼in), then press and stitch close to the edge. Turn the top of the bag to the inside about 6.5cm (2½in) to make a hem and channel for the drawstring and press. Stitch a line 5.5cm (2¼in) from the folded edge and another 4.5cm (1¾in) from the folded edge.

4 Cut fusible web the same size and shape as the prepared embroidery. With the web beneath, place the embroidery 2cm (¾in) from the bottom and sides of the bag and fuse. Sew or glue decorative trim along the raw edge of the embroidery starting and ending at centre bottom, attaching a rose where ends meet and at centre top.

5 Thread two 81cm (32in) lengths of ribbon through the casing in opposite directions to create a drawstring. Tack (baste) together each pair of ribbon ends 12.5cm (5in) from the cut ends. Attach a rose to hide the stitch. To finish, pull each end to gather.

You will need

* ✱ White 14-count Aida 23 x 23cm (9 x 9in)
* ✱ Tapestry needle size 24
* ✱ DMC stranded cotton (floss) as listed in chart key
* ✱ Kreinik blending filament #032 pearl
* ✱ Two pieces of fabric for bag 35.5 x 18cm (14 x 7in)
* ✱ Lightweight iron-on interfacing and fusible web
* ✱ 51cm (20in) length of decorative trim
* ✱ Four small satin roses
* ✱ Permanent fabric glue
* ✱ 2m (2yd) x 6mm (¼in) wide ribbon to tone with threads

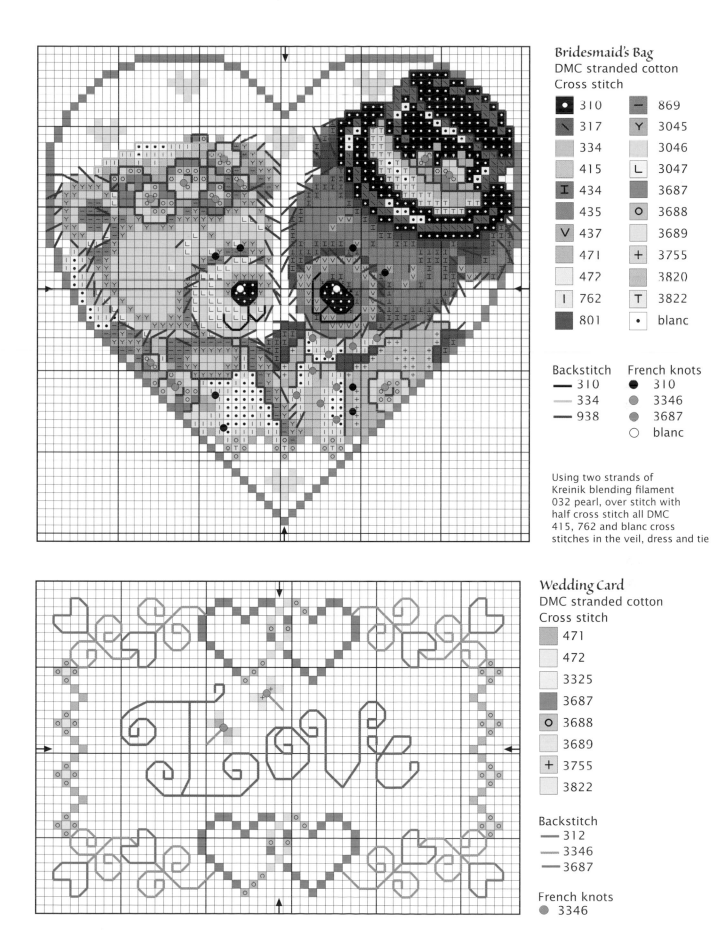

Bridesmaid's Bag
DMC stranded cotton
Cross stitch

Symbol	Colour	Symbol	Colour
●	310	−	869
\	317	Y	3045
	334		3046
	415	L	3047
I	434		3687
	435	O	3688
V	437		3689
	471	+	3755
	472		3820
I	762	T	3822
	801	•	blanc

Backstitch
— 310
— 334
— 938

French knots
● 310
● 3346
● 3687
○ blanc

Using two strands of
Kreinik blending filament
032 pearl, over stitch with
half cross stitch all DMC
415, 762 and blanc cross
stitches in the veil, dress and tie

Wedding Card
DMC stranded cotton
Cross stitch

Symbol	Colour
	471
	472
	3325
	3687
O	3688
	3689
+	3755
	3822

Backstitch
— 312
— 3346
— 3687

French knots
● 3346

Using two strands of
Kreinik blending filament
032 pearl, over stitch with
half cross stitch all DMC
415, 762 and blanc cross
stitches in veil, dress and tie

Backstitch
— 310
| | 312
| | 334
— 938
— 3346
— 3687

French knots
● 310
● 3346
● 3687
○ blanc

To change the names and
date on the sampler, use
the backstitch alphabet
on page 61

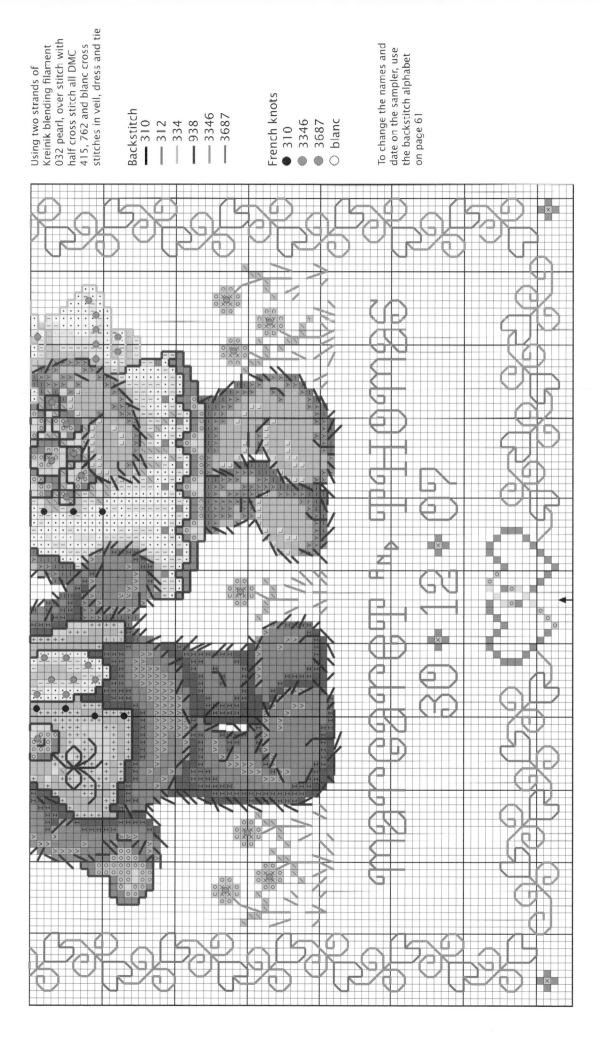

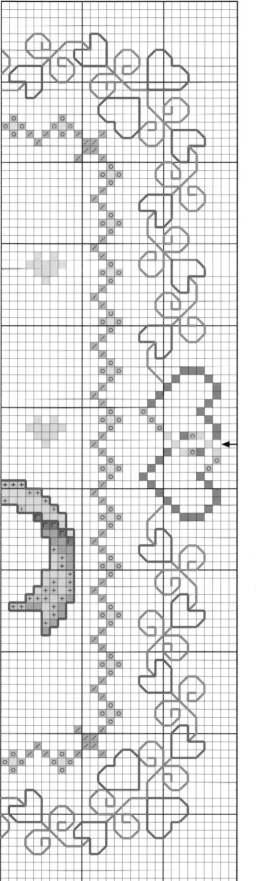

Ring Pillow
DMC stranded cotton

Cross stitch

Γ	312	o	3688
	334		3689
/	471	+	3755
	472	×	3820
	3325		3822
	3687		

Backstitch
— 312
— 3346
— 3687

French knots
● 3346

Change the names and date on the ring pillow
and sampler using this backstitch alphabet

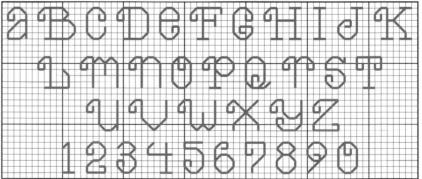

Designed by
Lesley Teare

Little Angels

The sweet innocence of childhood is captured in the six
utterly charming designs in this chapter. You are sure to
recognize some of these little sweethearts, whether it is the
shy little star, pretty as pink in her ballet outfit; the muddy
but triumphant sportsman; the nervous shepherd in his first
school play; the fairy unimpressed by her glittering ensemble or
the keen little helpers who are sometimes more of a hindrance.
The designs are all a similar size and have been made up in
various ways – as pictures, drawstring bags,
a nightdress case and an album
cover but there are many
more ways that you could
use them – see suggestions
throughout the chapter.

Little Star Bag

This gorgeous shoe bag (shown on the previous page) is trimmed with broderie anglaise and would be ideal for a little star's ballet or tap shoes, or to store a much-loved collection of toys.

Stitch count
95h x 66w
✳
Design size
17.3 x 12cm (6¾ x 4¾in)
✳
Finished bag size
33 x 25.5cm (13 x 10in)
including trim

1 Prepare for work referring to page 98 if necessary. Mark the centre of the fabric and centre of the chart on page 70. Mount your fabric in an embroidery frame if you wish.

2 Begin stitching from the centre of the fabric and chart and work outwards over one block. Work the full and three-quarter cross stitches using two strands of stranded cotton (floss) but one strand for DMC 3072 pale grey. Work backstitches with one strand.

3 Stitch the beads on to the hair and the glass treasures on the background fabric using a beading needle and matching thread.

4 Once all stitching is complete, make up into a drawstring bag as described in steps 3–5 on page 32 but adding the broderie anglaise trim as you sew the bottom seam.

You will need

* ✳ White 14-count Aida 25.5 x 20cm (10 x 8in)
* ✳ Tapestry needle size 24 and a beading needle
* ✳ DMC stranded cotton (floss) as listed in the chart key
* ✳ Mill Hill Glass Treasures, 12233 pale mauve
* ✳ Mill Hill Petite glass beads, 42018 pale pink
* ✳ Two pieces of broderie anglaise or cotton fabric for the bag, each 38 x 28cm (15 x 11in)
* ✳ Broderie anglaise frill 0.75m (1yd) long
* ✳ Iron-on interfacing
* ✳ Narrow ribbon or cord 1m (1yd) for drawstring
* ✳ Matching sewing thread

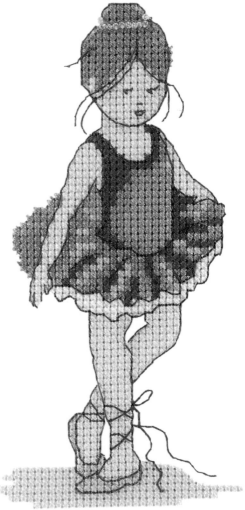

Cute Sentiment

Little Champ Bag

This shoe bag is simple to make and ideal for your little champ's sports kit. For maximum usefulness make the bag from denim or other sturdy, hardwearing fabric.

Stitch count
96h x 68w
✳
Design size
17.5 x 12.3cm (6¾ x 4¾in)
✳
Finished bag size
30.5 x 25.5cm (12 x 10in)

You will need

✳ White 14-count Aida 30.5 x 25.5cm (12 x 10in)
✳ Tapestry needle size 24
✳ DMC stranded cotton (floss) as listed in the chart key
✳ DMC Light Effects thread E317
✳ Two pieces of fabric for the bag, each 38 x 28cm (15 x 11in)
✳ Iron-on interfacing
✳ Cord 1m (1yd) for drawstring
✳ Matching sewing thread

1 Prepare for work referring to page 98 if necessary. Mark the centre of the fabric and centre of the chart on page 73. Mount your fabric in an embroidery frame if you wish.

2 Begin stitching from the centre of the fabric and chart and work outwards over one block. Work the full and three-quarter cross stitches using two strands of stranded cotton (floss) or metallic thread and backstitches with one strand.

3 Once all stitching is complete follow steps 3–5 on page 32 for making up into a drawstring bag.

Cute Sentiment

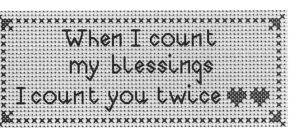

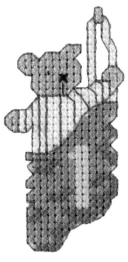

Little Fairy Nightdress Case

This lovely design is perfect to decorate a nightdress case. With its glistening metallic threads and glass beads it is sure to find favour for the little fairy in your life. The little shepherd design on page 68 could be used for a pyjama case.

1 Prepare for work referring to page 98 if necessary. Mark the centre of the fabric and centre of the chart on page 71. Mount your fabric in an embroidery frame if you wish.

2 Begin stitching from the centre of the fabric and chart and work outwards over one block. Work the full and three-quarter cross stitches using two strands of stranded cotton (floss). Use one strand of DMC stranded cotton 3078 and one strand of Glissen Gloss 303 together in the needle. Use two strands of Glissen Gloss 301. Work French knots with two strands of thread wound twice around the needle. Work backstitches with one strand. Sew the beads in place on the stitched design using a beading needle and matching thread (see page 100).

3 Once all stitching is complete, make up into a nightdress case as follows. Trim the embroidery, leaving eight squares of Aida outside the stitched area. Fold four squares under and press with an iron. Now cut three pieces of cotton fabric or broderie anglaise 32 x 26.5cm (12½ x 10½in). Using matching thread, sew the embroidery to the front of one of the pieces of fabric.

4 With the fabric right side up, tack (baste) a line 1.25cm (½in) from the edge and tack the frill to this line. Make a fold of 10cm (4in) on the right side of each of the other two pieces of fabric on the shorter sides of each, neatening edges by oversewing. Place these on top of each other, right sides together, to make an opening and then place both pieces on top of the front piece of fabric, right sides together (as in an Oxford-type case). Tack and machine with matching thread 1.25cm (½in) from the edges. Mitre the corners and turn the case right side out.

5 To finish, attach the ribbon bows to the corners of the stitched design and the corners of the case with matching or invisible thread.

Stitch count
91h x 66w
✻
Design size
16.5 x 12cm (6½ x 4¾in)

You will need

* ✻ White 14-count Aida 25.5 x 20cm (10 x 8in)
* ✻ Tapestry needle size 24 and a beading needle
* ✻ DMC stranded cotton (floss) as listed in the chart key
* ✻ Madeira Glissen Gloss thread, 303 pale yellow and 301 rainbow
* ✻ Mill Hill glass beads, 00143 pale blue
* ✻ Cotton or broderie anglaise fabric 0.5m (½yd)
* ✻ Broderie anglaise frill 1.5m (1¾yd) long
* ✻ Eight small ribbon bows
* ✻ Matching sewing thread

More Cute Ideas...

Make a useful coat hook rack by stitching the teddies from the chart on page 71 repeatedly along a length of Aida band. Iron interfacing on the back of the embroidery and then use strong craft glue to fix it to a piece of wood. Screw coat hooks through the Aida band into the wood.

Little Helper Pictures

These sweet little pictures would be wonderful for a toddler's room and could be worked as a set. If desired, you could backstitch a child's name in place of the 'Little Helper' words using the alphabet on page 72.

Stitch count 95h x 68w (for each picture)
✳
Design size 17.3 x 12.3cm (6¾ x 4¾in)

1 Prepare for work referring to page 98 if necessary. Mark the centre of the fabric and centre of the chart on page 72 or page 75. Mount your fabric in an embroidery frame if you wish.

2 Begin stitching from the centre of the fabric and chart and work outwards over one block. Work the full and three-quarter cross stitches using two strands of stranded cotton (floss). Work French knots with two strands of thread wound twice around the needle. Work backstitches with one strand.

3 Once all the stitching is complete, finish your picture by mounting in a suitable frame (see page 102 for advice).

You will need
(for each picture)

✳ White 14-count Aida 30.5 x 25.5cm (12 x 10in)

✳ Tapestry needle size 24

✳ DMC stranded cotton (floss) as listed in the chart key

✳ Suitable picture frame

Little Shepherd Album

Stitch count
96h x 68w
✳
Design size
17.5 x 12.3cm (6¾ x 4¾in)

This delightful design makes a wonderful decoration for an album. Follow the chart and key on page 74 and work on white 14-count Aida, using two strands of stranded cotton (floss) for full and three-quarter cross stitches (but one strand for metallic stitches) and one strand for backstitches. Once stitching is complete, trim the embroidery to fit your album and fringe the edges by pulling out a few threads all round. Stick to the album using double-sided tape. To use the design to embellish a pyjama case, simply follow the case making up instructions in steps 3–5 on page 66 but replace the broderie anglaise trim with either decorative cord or a boldly patterned ribbon trim.

Little Star Bag
DMC stranded cotton
Cross stitch

- 209
- 601
- 602
- 603
- 604
- 605
- 747
- 818
- 963
- 3072 (1 strand)
- 3828
- 3855
- blanc

Backstitch
— 601
— 869

Mill Hill
petite beads
42018
pale pink

Mill Hill
glass treasures
12233
pale mauve

Little Fairy Nightdress Case
DMC stranded cotton
Cross stitch

▨	420
▨	729
▨	761
▨	818
╱	3713
❘	3761
▨	3766
▨	E3821 Light Effects

▨	DMC 3078 + 303 Glissen Gloss (1 strand of each together in needle)
▨	301 Glissen Gloss (2 strands)

Backstitch
— 597
— 602
— 869

French knots
● 869

Mill Hill glass seed beads
◉ 00143 pale blue

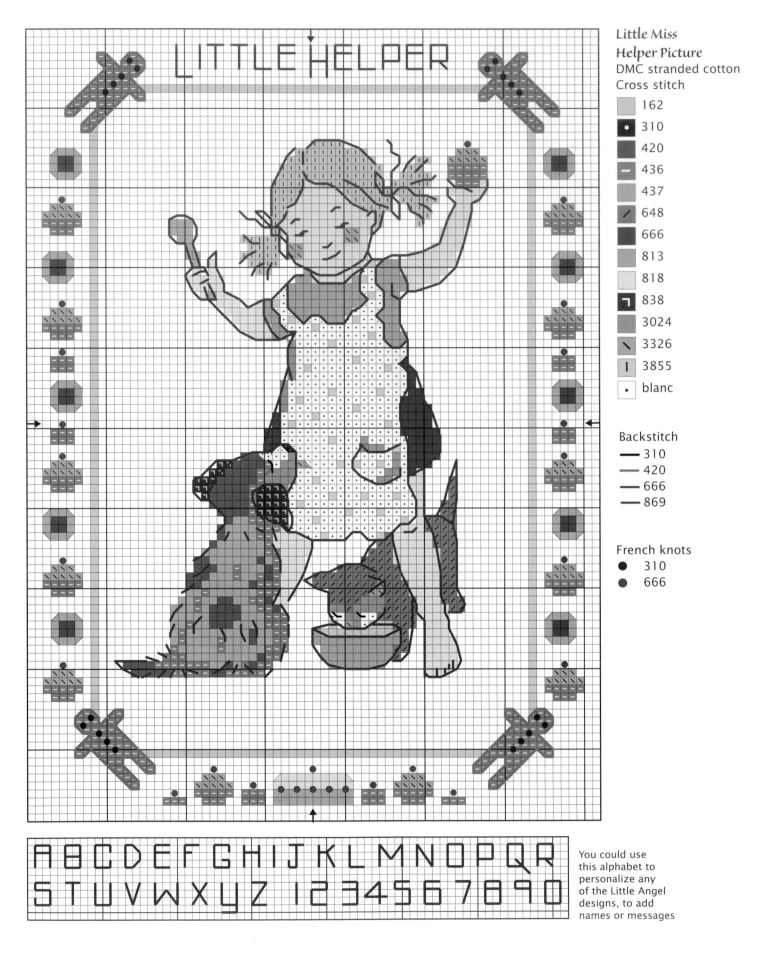

Little Miss
Helper Picture
DMC stranded cotton
Cross stitch

	162
	310
	420
	436
	437
	648
	666
	813
	818
	838
	3024
	3326
	3855
	blanc

Backstitch
— 310
— 420
— 666
— 869

French knots
● 310
● 666

You could use
this alphabet to
personalize any
of the Little Angel
designs, to add
names or messages

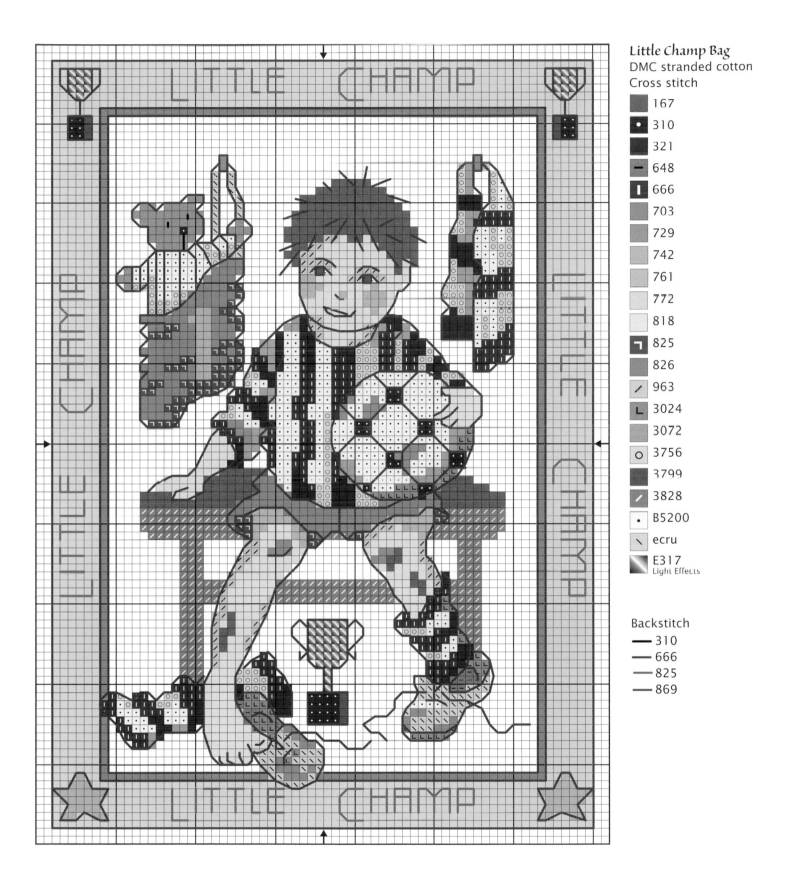

Little Champ Bag
DMC stranded cotton
Cross stitch

	167
●	310
	321
−	648
I	666
	703
	729
	742
	761
	772
	818
⌐	825
	826
/	963
L	3024
	3072
○	3756
	3799
/	3828
•	B5200
\	ecru
	E317 Light Effects

Backstitch
—— 310
—— 666
—— 825
—— 869

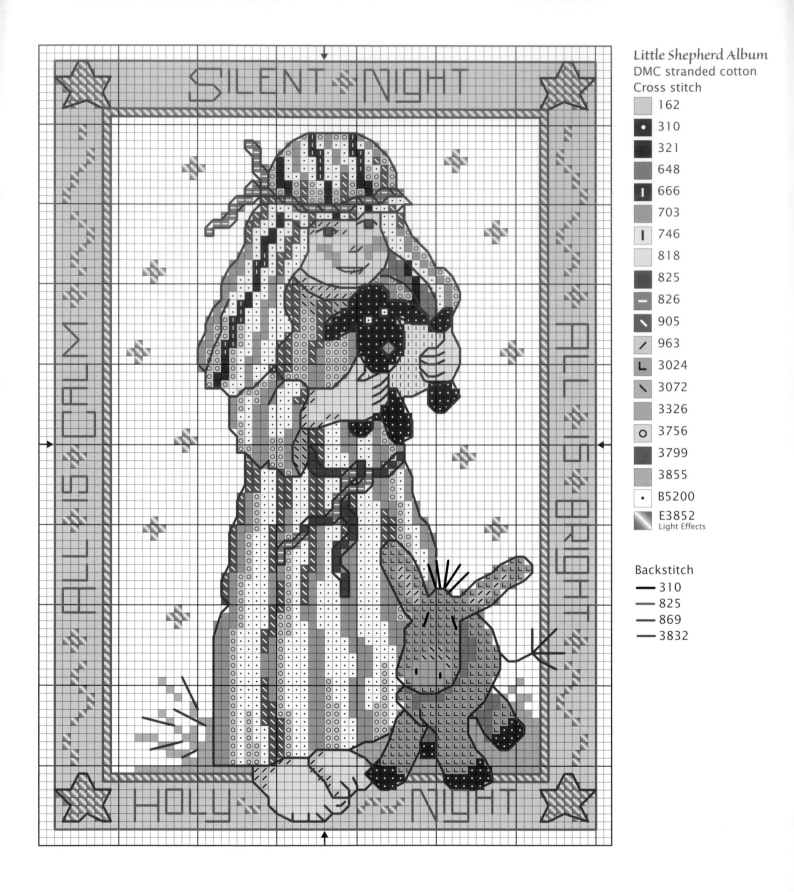

Little Shepherd Album
DMC stranded cotton
Cross stitch

	162
●	310
	321
	648
I	666
	703
I	746
	818
	825
−	826
＼	905
／	963
L	3024
＼	3072
	3326
○	3756
	3799
	3855
•	B5200
	E3852 Light Effects

Backstitch
— 310
— 825
— 869
— 3832

Little Helper Picture
DMC stranded cotton
Cross stitch

Symbol	Colour
V	164
■	310
	666
	703
	729
	742
\	746
	761
	772
I	813
	818
⌐	825
	826
/	963
	3072
	3325

Backstitch
—— 310
—— 666
—— 869

Designed by

Joan Elliott

It's a Dog's Life

It is said that as time goes by, dogs and their owners begin to look alike.
Picture the pampered poodle strutting down the city boulevard with her
sophisticated owner, the drowsy basset hound and his sleepy-eyed friend
waiting in line at the local coffee shop, or the woolly sheepdog
and his windblown chum out for a bracing walk.
With a tilt of the head and a soulful expression, these
beloved companions seem to embody human
characteristics so perfectly. The six dog breeds featured in
this chapter are a whimsical interpretation of
some of our everyday frustrations and
challenges. From coping with a bad
hair day, to a quick solution for getting
what you want, these furry
friends say it all.

Dog's Life Pictures

Friends and family alike are sure to love these amusing dog designs – see below and opposite for other ideas on using the designs.

Stitch count (each picture) 88h x 60w
✻
Design size 16 x 10.9cm (6¼ x 4¼in)

1 Prepare for work, referring to page 98 if necessary. Mark the centre of the fabric and centre of the chart (charts are on pages 80–86). Mount your fabric in an embroidery frame if you wish.

2 Start stitching from the centre of the chart and fabric and work outwards over one block. Use one strand for Kreinik cross stitches in the poodle design. Use two strands of stranded cotton (floss) for all other full and three-quarter cross stitches. Work all French knots using two strands wound once around the needle. Following the chart colours, use one strand for all backstitches and for long stitches.

3 Once all the stitching is complete, finish your picture by mounting and framing (see advice on page 102).

More Cute Ideas...

Make up these adorable dog designs in a variety of different ways to send love and affection to those near and dear to you – they're sure to get the message!

With a gift of a flower and eyes full of love, who could resist this darling? Stitch the design on 18-count Aida to create a smaller picture and mount it in a card to send love to someone dear.

Filled with energy and ready to take on the world, this cute little one is ready to let everyone know who is boss. Stitch this design as a cheeky desk sign for a favourite colleague or boss.

With messy hair and scruffy looks, don't bother trying to tidy up this adorable creature, just let his free spirit soar. Work the design and glue it to a journal cover for a budding young Einstein to keep his notes.

Peaking from under the bed covers with droopy eyes, this sleepy soul needs more than one coffee to start the day. To warn others you are not at your best in the morning, stitch the design on 18-count Aida and use fusible web to attach it to a dressing gown.

Clipped and trimmed and wearing gold accessories, this haughty lady doesn't hesitate to let others know where she stands. This design would be perfect made up into a teasing door sign for a self-absorbed teenage girl.

When the wind is howling and leaves are swirling, this shaggy companion will just chalk it off as another bad hair day! Work this design for a tousled friend and attach it to a ready-made bag – perfect for their hair-styling necessities.

Poodle
DMC stranded cotton
Cross stitch

⊡	310
	318
╱	415
T	601
	602
–	603
	605
○	762
•	blanc
◩	Kreinik #4 braid 028 citron (1 strand)

Backstitch/
Long stitch
—— 310
—— 601

French knots
● 601

Mutt
DMC stranded cotton
Cross stitch

⊡	310
V	317
	318
╱	415
T	601
	602
	746
	869
	906
✗	3045
	3046
L	3047

Backstitch/
Long stitch
—— 310
—— 601

French knots
● 310
● 601
○ blanc

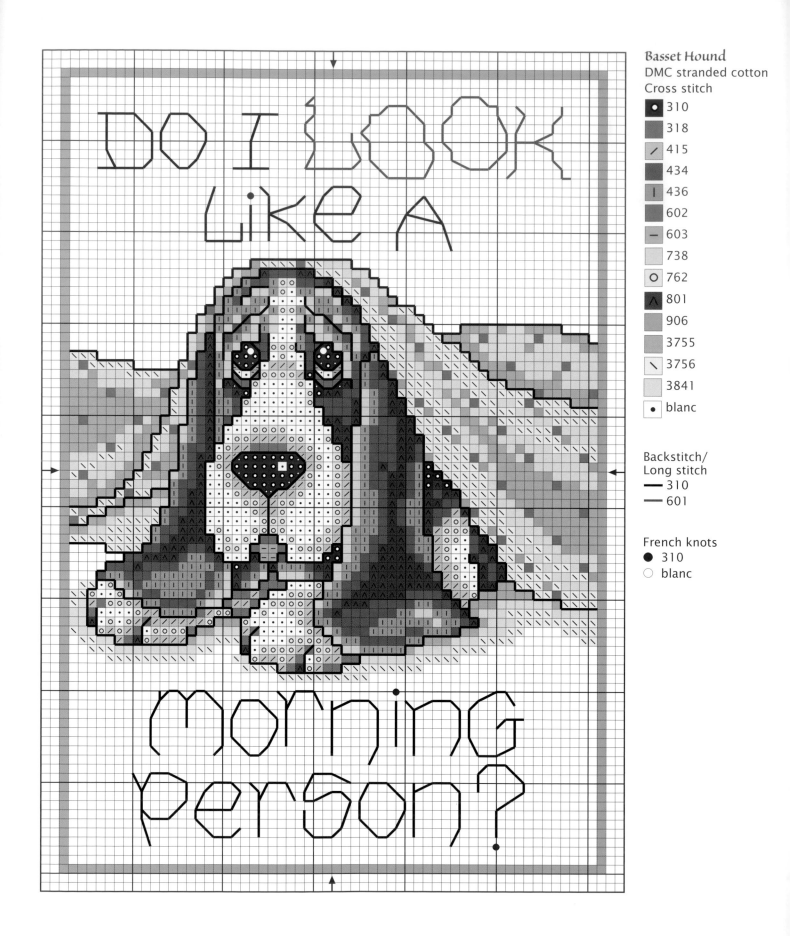

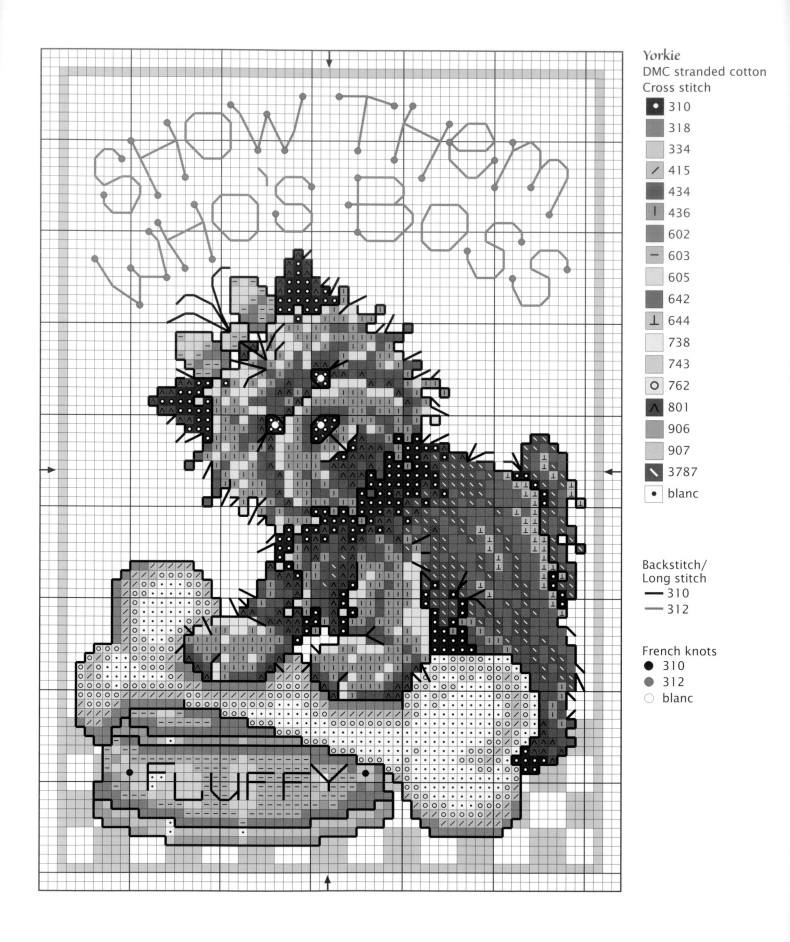

Yorkie
DMC stranded cotton
Cross stitch

Symbol	Colour
⊡	310
	318
	334
╱	415
	434
I	436
	602
−	603
	605
	642
⊥	644
	738
	743
O	762
∧	801
	906
	907
╲	3787
•	blanc

Backstitch/
Long stitch
—— 310
—— 312

French knots
● 310
● 312
○ blanc

Spaniel
DMC stranded cotton
Cross stitch

	310
	312
	334
/	415
	434
I	436
	602
–	603
	738
	742
	743
O	762
∧	801
	906
	907
•	blanc

Backstitch/
Long stitch
—— 310
—— 312
—— 601

French knots
● 312

DMC stranded cotton
Cross stitch

- ⊡ 310
- V 317
- 318
- ╱ 415
- 434
- O 762
- 906
- 907
- • blanc

Backstitch/
Long stitch
— 310
— 334
— 601

French knots
● 601

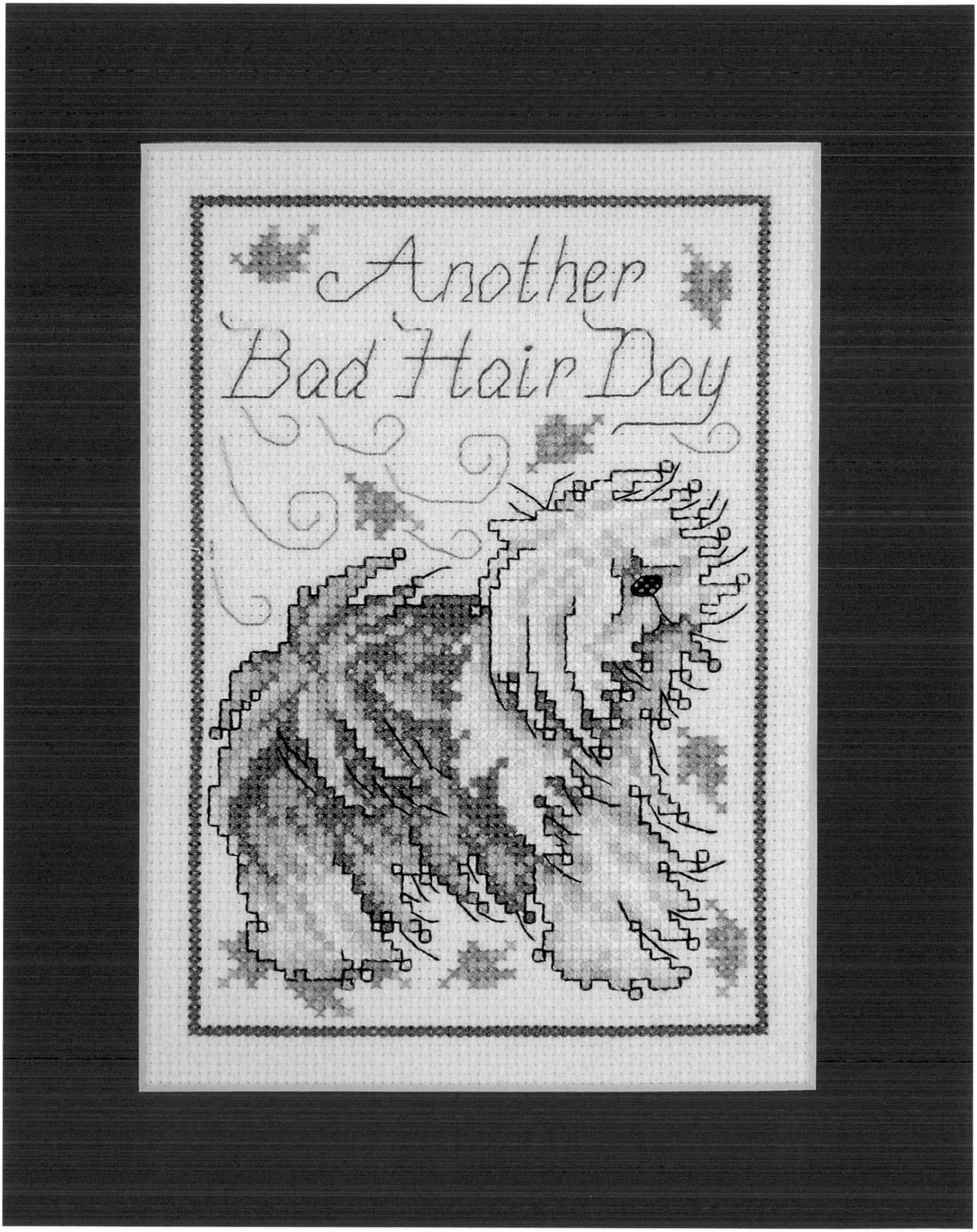
Another
Bad Hair Day

Christmas Cuties

Designed by
Ursula Michael

Christmas time is filled with memorable images – adorable angels, cuddly teddy bears and pretty fairies and elves. This chapter brings you tubby Santas and playful snow babies and ideas on how to use these fun designs. The welcoming Christmas banner shown opposite has five musical Santas, each framed by festive fabric and linked together with satin bows. The framed picture features sweet snow babies wishing for snow and ready to play. The use of metallic thread brings an extra sparkle to the design. If you prefer, you could work the Santas and snow babies individually to create a wide range of Christmas cards and little gifts.

Santas' Greetings Banner

This colourful banner is sure to get you in the mood for the festive season. If preferred, the complete Santa design charted on pages 94–95 could be framed as a picture instead. Or why not work the individual designs to create all sorts of smaller projects?

Stitch count
Whole design 83h x 219w
Individual Santas 55h x 49w

✳

Design size
Whole design
15 x 40cm (6 x 15½in)
Individual Santas
10 x 9cm (4 x 3½in) maximum

✳

Finished size of banner
15 x 68.5cm (6 x 27in)

You will need

* ✳ Five pieces of white
  14-count Aida
  23 x 23cm (9 x 9in)
* ✳ Tapestry needle size 26
* ✳ DMC stranded cotton (floss)
  as listed in the chart key
* ✳ Kreinik #4 braid, 003 red
* ✳ Red fabric 0.25m (¼yd)
  x 112cm (44in) wide
* ✳ Fast2Fuse double-sided
  fusible interfacing
* ✳ Red satin ribbon 3.75m
  (4yd) x 2cm (¾in) wide
* ✳ Matching sewing thread

1 Prepare for work, referring to page 98 if necessary. Mark the centre of the fabric and centre of the chart (pages 94–95). Mount your fabric in an embroidery frame if you wish.

2 Begin stitching from the centre of the fabric and chart and work outwards over one block. Use two strands of stranded cotton (floss) for full and quarter cross stitches. (Note: in this design quarter cross stitches are shown on the chart as a triangle.) Use one strand for Kreinik cross stitches. Use one strand of thread for all backstitches.

3 Once all the stitching is complete, make each Santa up as follows. Trim the excess Aida 3cm (1⅛in) from the motif on all sides. Cut the red fabric into strips 3.2 x 16.5cm (1¼ x 6½in), allowing four strips for each Santa. Place the left and right side borders 1.25cm (½in) from the stitched area, right sides together and machine sew the seams. Repeat for top and bottom borders (see diagram below).

Framing a Santa design by sewing border strips around it – side strips first, followed by top and bottom strips

4 Cut a red backing piece the same size as the front. Place right sides together and machine sew the top and two side seams, leaving the bottom edge open. Trim corners. Cut fusible interfacing 3mm (⅛in) smaller than the Aida. Turn the Santa inside out and slip the interfacing inside the pocket. Tuck the bottom raw edge inside and hand sew the opening closed. Press the Santa on the front and back to fuse the interfacing. Repeat for all five Santas.

5 To join the Santas into a banner, arrange them in a row. Sew the top corners together with red thread. Make small red bows from the satin ribbon and sew one to each corner. Finish by tacking a 46cm (18in) length of ribbon to each end corner to hang the banner.

Cute Sentiment

More Cute Ideas...

Make a set of festive table mats by stitching a single Santa in the corner of a piece of white or pale-coloured 28-count linen. Stitch the design over two fabric threads, adding a border if desired (see the Cute Sentiments throughout the book for ideas on borders). When finished, turn a small hem all round and press.

Santa Card

A marching Santa announces Christmas is here on this fun greetings card. Any of the Santa designs could be used on the card – or work all six for a great set of festive cards.

Stitch count
51h x 46w
✳
Design size
9.25 x 8.5cm (3¾ x 3¼in)

You will need

✳ White 14-count Aida 23 x 23cm (9 x 9in)

✳ Tapestry needle size 26

✳ DMC stranded cotton (floss) as listed in the chart key

✳ Lightweight fusible interfacing 15 x 15cm (6 x 6in)

✳ HeatnBond adhesive (see Suppliers), or other fabric adhesive

✳ Green fabric 20 x 20cm (8 x 8in)

✳ Red jumbo rickrack braid 0.5m (½yd)

✳ Acrylic star gems 5mm in a mix of red, gold and green

✳ Tacky glue

✳ White card stock 18 x 35cm (7 x 14in)

✳ White organdie ribbon about 1m (1yd) long x 1.25cm (½in) wide

1 Prepare for work, referring to page 98 if necessary. Mark the centre of the fabric and centre of the charted motif.

2 Begin stitching from the centre of the fabric and motif following step 2 on page 90. Note: you will not need all of the colours for an individual Santa – check the chart before you buy.

3 Once all stitching is complete, make up as a card as follows. Stitch or glue the rickrack braid in a circle around the stitched motif. Place the fusible interfacing on the back of the work, press and trim the excess Aida fabric. Glue the stars on the embroidery as desired.

4 Make the card by applying the HeatnBond adhesive to the back of the green fabric following the manufacturer's instructions. Place the green fabric on the bottom half of the card stock, press and allow to cool. Trim the card to 16.5 x 33cm (6½ x 13in) and fold it in half. Glue the Santa to the fabric-covered front of the card. To finish, tie the ribbon to the top of the card.

More Cute Ideas...

Create a special gift for the Christmas cook by stitching a Santa on 14-count Aida, backing the embroidery with iron-on interfacing and fusing it to the front of a ready-made apron.

Let It Snow Picture

Stitching a cute snow babies picture (shown on page 89) will start the festive season in fun style. For a quicker project see the ornament below.

Stitch count 81h x 164w

✳

Design size 14.7 x 30cm (5¾ x 11¾in)

You will need

✳ White 14-count Aida 35 x 50cm (14 x 20in)

✳ Tapestry needle size 26

✳ DMC stranded cotton (floss) as listed in the chart key

✳ Kreinik #4 braid, 3214 blue zircon

✳ Suitable picture frame

1 Prepare for work, referring to page 98 if necessary. Mark the centre of the fabric and centre of the chart on pages 96–97. Mount your fabric in an embroidery frame if you wish.

2 Begin stitching from the centre of the fabric and chart and work outwards over one block. Use two strands of stranded cotton (floss) for full and quarter cross stitches. (Note: quarter cross stitches are shown on the chart as a triangle.) Use one strand for Kreinik cross stitches. Use one strand for all backstitches.

3 Once all the stitching is complete, mount and frame as a picture – see page 102 for advice.

Snow Baby Ornament

Stitch just one of the snow babies as a pretty ornament to hang on the Christmas tree – or work all five as a delightful set. Work the design on white 14-count Aida and use the chart and key on page 96–97. Use two strands of stranded cotton (floss)

Stitch count
57h x 39w maximum

✳

Design size
10 x 7cm (4 x 2¾in)

for full and quarter cross stitches and one strand for backstitches. Note: you will not need all of the colours for an individual snow baby – check the key before you buy. Make up as an ornament as follows. Trim the embroidery to about 12.7 x 10cm (5 x 4in) and cut another piece of white fabric the same size. Sandwich double-sided fusible interfacing between the white fabric and the Aida and press on both sides to fuse together. Trim excess fabric around the stitched area. Finish by folding some narrow ribbon in half and glue to the top back of the ornament.

Left

Santas' Greetings Banner
DMC stranded cotton
Cross stitch

⊙ 310	┃ 351	╱ 703	● 816	╱ 3752	▎3820
▓ 349	▓ 353	▓ 726	∨ 3033	3756	• blanc
	▓ 434				
	▓ 701				

Backstitch
— 310
— Kreinik #4 braid
003 red

Right

Let It Snow Picture
DMC stranded cotton

Cross stitch

● 310	▨ 704	✚ 799
▨ 321	▨ 726	▨ 816
▨ 353	▨ 798	Ⅰ 958

○ 964	▨ 3755	╲ 3841
╱ 970	∧ 3801	• blanc
▨ 986	— 3820	▨ Kreinik #4 braid 3214 blue zircon (1 strand)

Backstitch

— 310

— Kreinik #4 braid 3214 blue zircon

Materials and Techniques

This section describes the materials and equipment you need to complete the projects in this book, followed by the stitches required. For beginners there are some handy tips for perfect stitching.

Materials

Fabrics

The fabrics used for counted cross stitch, mainly Aidas and evenweaves, are woven so they have the same number of threads or blocks to 2.5cm (1in) in both directions. They are available in different counts – the higher the count, the more threads or stitches to 2.5cm (1in), and the finer the fabric.

Aida This is ideal for the beginner because the fabric threads are woven in blocks rather than singly. It is available in many fibres, colours and counts and as different width bands. When stitching on Aida, one block on the fabric corresponds to one square on a chart and generally cross stitch is worked over *one block*.

Evenweaves These are made from various fibres including linen, cotton and acrylic. Evenweaves are woven singly and are available in different colours, counts and bands. To even out any oddities in the weave, cross stitch is usually worked over *two threads* of the fabric.

Threads

The most commonly used thread for cross stitch is stranded cotton (floss). The DMC range has been used by the designers in this book but if you prefer the Anchor range ask about a conversion table at your local needlecraft store.

Some of the projects feature metallic threads for extra sparkle: these include threads from the Kreinik range, DMC Light Effects and Madeira Glissen Gloss. The project instructions tell you how many strands of each thread to use.

Beads

Many of the designs in the book use beads to bring an extra sparkle and dimension to the cross stitch. If you want to use beads as an embellishment there are many types and colours to choose from. Some Mill Hill glass seed beads and crystal treasures were used in this book. See page 100 for how to attach beads.

Tools

There are many tools and gadgets available for embroidery in craft shops but you really only need the following.

Needles Use blunt tapestry needles for counted cross stitch. The most common sizes used are 24 and 26 but the size depends on the project you are working on and personal preference. Avoid leaving a needle in the fabric unless it is gold plated or it may cause marks. A beading needle (or fine 'sharp' needle), which is much thinner, will be needed to attach seed beads.

Scissors Use dressmaker's shears for cutting fabric and a small, sharp pair of pointed scissors for cutting embroidery threads.

Frames and hoops These are not essential but if you use one, choose one large enough to hold the complete design to avoid marking the fabric and flattening stitches.

Basic Techniques

Preparing Fabric for Work

Press embroidery fabric before you begin stitching and trim the selvedge or any rough edges. Work from the middle of the fabric and middle of the chart to ensure your design is centred on the fabric. Find the middle of the fabric by folding it in four and pressing lightly. Mark the folds with tailor's chalk or tacking (basting) stitches following a fabric thread. When working with linen sew a narrow hem around all raw edges to preserve them for finishing later.

Stitch Count and Design Size

Each project gives details of the stitch count and finished design size but if you wish to work the design on a different count fabric you will need to be able to calculate the finished size. To do this, count the number of stitches across the height and width of the design and divide this by the fabric count number, e.g., 140 stitches x 140 stitches ÷ by 14-count = a design size of 10 x 10in (25.4 x 25.4cm). Remember that working on evenweave usually means working over two threads not one, so divide the fabric count by two before you start.

Using the Charts

The designs in this book are worked from colour charts, with symbols where necessary. Each square, both occupied and unoccupied, represents one block of Aida or two threads of evenweave. Each occupied square equals one stitch. Some designs use three-quarter cross stitches, shown as a triangle within a grid square. (The Christmas Cuties charts use a quarter cross stitch instead of a three-quarter cross stitch.) Some designs use French knots and beads and these are labelled in the key.

Starting and Finishing Stitching

Unless indicated otherwise, begin stitching in the middle of a design to ensure an adequate margin for making up. Start and finish stitching neatly, avoiding knots as they can create lumps.

Knotless loop start This neat start can be used with an *even* number of strands i.e., 2, 4 or 6. To stitch with two strands, begin with one strand about 80cm (30in). Double it and thread the needle with the two ends. Put the needle up through the fabric from the wrong side, where you intend to begin stitching, leaving the loop at the back. Form a half cross stitch, put the needle back through the fabric and through the loop. With the thread anchored you can begin.

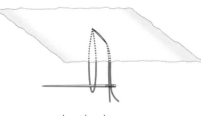

A knotless loop start

Away waste knot start Start this way if using an *odd* number of strands or when tweeding threads (i.e., mixing thread types or colours). Thread your needle with the number of strands required and knot the end. Insert the needle into the right side of the fabric some way away from where you wish to begin stitching. Stitch towards the knot and cut it off when the threads are anchored. Alternatively, snip off the knot, thread

the needle and work under a few stitches to anchor the tail.

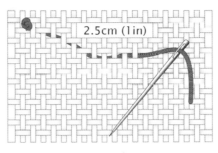

An away waste knot start

Finishing stitching At the back of the work, pass the needle and thread under several stitches of the same or similar colour, and then snip off the loose end close to the stitching. You can begin a new colour in a similar way.

Working the Stitches
Backstitch

Backstitch is used for outlining a design or part of a design, to add detail or emphasis, or for lettering. It is added after the cross stitch has been completed so the backstitch line isn't broken by cross stitches. It is shown on charts by solid coloured lines.

Follow the numbered sequence in the diagram below, working the stitches over one block of Aida or over two threads of evenweave, unless stated otherwise on the chart.

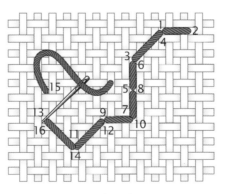

Backstitch

Cross Stitch

This is the most commonly used stitch in this book and it can be worked singly or in two journeys. For neat stitching, keep the top stitch facing the same direction. Half cross stitch is simply a single diagonal line.

Cross stitch on Aida Cross stitch on Aida fabric is normally worked over one block of the fabric. To work a complete cross stitch, follow the numbered sequence in the diagram below: bring the needle up through the fabric at 1, cross one block of the fabric and insert the needle at 2. Push the needle through and bring it up at 3, ready to complete the stitch at 4. To work the adjacent stitch, bring the needle up at the bottom right-hand corner of the first stitch.

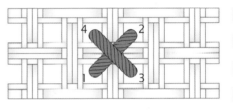

Single cross stitch on Aida fabric

To work cross stitches in two journeys, work the first leg of the cross stitch as above but instead of completing the stitch, work the adjacent half stitch and continue on to the end of the row. Complete all the crosses by working the other diagonals on the return journey.

Cross stitch in two journeys on Aida fabric

Cross stitch on evenweave

Cross stitch on evenweave is usually worked over two fabric threads in each direction to even out oddities in the thickness of the fibres. Bring the needle up to the left of a vertical thread and work cross stitch in two directions, in a sewing movement, half cross stitch in one direction and then work back and cover the original stitches with the second row.

This forms neat vertical lines on the back and somewhere to finish off raw ends.

Single cross stitch on evenweave

Three-quarter Cross Stitch

Three-quarter cross stitch is a fractional stitch that can produce the illusion of curves. It can be formed on Aida or evenweave but is more successful on evenweave. These stitches are shown on charts as a triangle (half square).

Work the first half of a cross stitch as usual. Work the second 'quarter' stitch over the top and down into the central hole to anchor the first half of the stitch. If using Aida, push the needle through the centre of a fabric block. Where two three-quarter stitches lie back-to-back in the space of one full cross stitch, work both of the respective quarter stitches into the central hole.

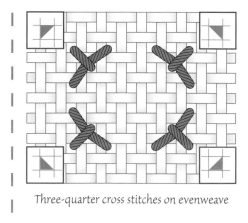

Three-quarter cross stitches on evenweave

French Knot

French knots are small stitches predominantly used for eyes and to add detail to a design. They are shown on the charts as coloured circles, with the thread code in the key.

Bring the needle through to the front of the fabric and wind the thread around the needle twice. Begin to push the needle partly through to the back, one thread or part of a block away from the entry point. (This will stop the stitch being pulled to the wrong side.) Gently pull the thread you have wound so it sits snugly at the point where the needle enters the fabric. Pull the needle through to the back and you should have a perfect knot in position. For bigger French knots, it is best to add more strands of thread to the needle rather than winding more times.

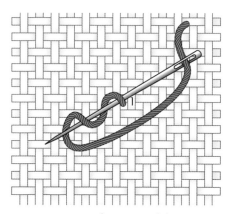

Starting to form a French knot

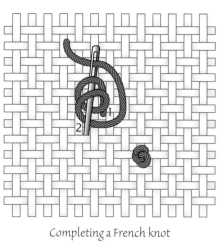

Completing a French knot

Long Stitch

Long straight stitches are used in some of the designs. They are very simple to stitch and can be worked on any fabric.

To work long stitch, simply bring the needle and thread up where the stitch is to start, at 1 in the diagram below, and down where the chart indicates it should finish, at 2.

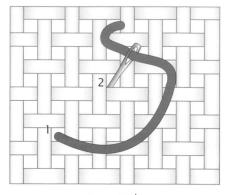

Long stitch

Working with Beads

Beads, especially seed beads, make a wonderful embellishment to cross stitch. Beads are shown on the charts as a large coloured circle, with details of the bead type and code in the key.

Attach beads using a beading needle or very fine 'sharp' needle, thread that matches the bead colour and a half cross stitch. To ensure beads stay firmly in position, make an extra little stitch at the back of the work after sewing each bead.

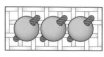

Attaching beads

Making Up

The cross stitch designs in this book have been made up in different ways, including pictures, cushions, drawstring bags and book covers – and the making up instructions are given within the relevant project. Two general techniques, framing a picture and mounting work in cards, are described here. There are also many 'More Cute Ideas' throughout the book, suggesting other ways to use the designs and display your work.

Mounting Work in Cards

Many of the smaller designs in the book would make great greetings cards and there are suggestions for taking smaller parts of the designs to stitch as cards. There are many card blanks available from craft shops and mail-order suppliers (see page 104) and you can also make your own cards. The instructions below describe how to make a card with a small, square window (aperture) – simply change the dimensions to suit the embroidery you wish to display.

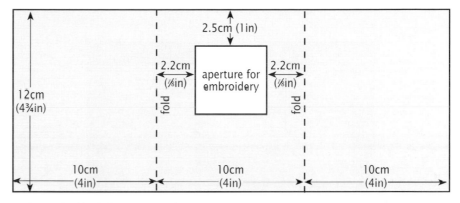

Making a double-fold aperture card

Making a Double-Fold Card with Aperture

1 Choose a card colour to complement your embroidery and cut a piece 30 x 12cm (12 x 4¾in) (see diagram above). On the wrong side of the card, draw two lines dividing it into three sections of 10cm (4in). Score gently along each line with the back of a craft knife to make folding easier.

2 In the centre section, mark an aperture slightly bigger than the finished size of the design – the diagram shows an aperture of about 5.7 x 5.7cm (2¼ x 2¼in), with a border of about 2.2cm (⅞in) along the top and sides. Cut out the aperture with a sharp craft knife, cutting into the corners neatly. Trim the left edge of the first section by 2mm (⅛in) so it lies flat when folded over to the inside. This will cover the back of the stitching. Fold the left and then the right section on the scored lines.

Mounting Work into a Double-Fold Card

1 Lay the card right side up on top of the design so the stitching is in the middle of the aperture. Place a pin in each corner and remove the card. Trim the fabric to within about 1.5cm (⅝in) so it fits into the card.

2 On the wrong side of the card, stick double-sided tape around the aperture and peel off the backing tape (some ready-made cards already have this tape in place). Place the card over the design, using the pins to guide the position. Press down firmly to stick the fabric to the card. Remove pins.

3 On the wrong side of the card, stick more double-sided tape around the edge of the middle section. Peel off the backing and fold the left section in to cover the back of the stitching, pressing down firmly.

Mounting Work into a Single-Fold Card

You can also mount your embroidery on a single-fold card. Trim the embroidery to the size required leaving two or three rows all round if you want a fringe. Pull away the outer fabric threads to form the fringe and use double-sided tape to attach the embroidery to the front of your card.

For a neat edge that does not fray, fuse iron-on adhesive to the back of the embroidery and trim the embroidery to size before fixing it to the front of your card.

Mounting and Framing a Picture

Many of the cross stitch embroideries in this book have been designed to make stunning pictures. You could take your work to a professional framer who will help you chose a suitable mount and frame for the design. Alternatively, you could mount the work yourself, using the following instructions and a ready-made frame.

You will need: a suitable picture frame; mount board the same size as the frame; wadding (batting); double-sided adhesive tape; pins and crochet cotton or strong thread.

1 Cut your mount board to the size of the picture frame aperture (draw around the sheet of glass). Cut a piece of wadding (batting) the same size and secure it to the mount board with double-sided tape. Lay your embroidery face up on the wadding (batting) and when you are happy with the position, push a line of pins down each side into the board. Check the stitching is straight and then trim the fabric to leave about 5cm (2in) all round.

2 Fold the excess fabric to the back. Thread a needle with a long length of crochet cotton or strong thread, knot the end and lace the two opposite sides together on the back, starting at one end and working in a zigzag manner. When you reach the other end, pull the lacing tight and adjust the laced threads one by one before finishing off. Repeat this process on the two remaining edges. Alternatively, you could use double-sided tape to secure the fabric to the back of the board.

3 Fold down the corners and stitch neatly into place. Remove the pins and assemble your work in its frame. It is not necessary to use the glass; this often flattens the stitches when they are pushed against it.

Perfect Stitching

✳ Organize your threads before you start a project as this will help to avoid confusion later. Put threads on an organizer (available from craft shops) and always include the manufacturer's name and the shade number.

✳ Separate the strands on a skein of stranded cotton (floss) before taking the number you need, realigning them and threading your needle.

✳ When stitching with metallic threads, work with shorter lengths, about 30cm (12in) to avoid tangling and excessive wear on the thread.

✳ If using a frame, try to avoid a hoop as it will stretch the fabric and leave a mark that may be difficult to remove.

✳ Plan your route carefully around the chart, counting over short distances where possible to avoid making mistakes.

✳ Work your cross stitch in two directions in a sewing movement – half cross stitch in one direction and then cover those original stitches with the second row. This forms vertical lines on the back and gives somewhere to finish off raw ends tidily. For neat work the top stitches should all face the same direction.

✳ If adding a backstitch outline, always add it after the cross stitch has been completed to prevent the solid line of the backstitch being broken.

The Designers

Claire Crompton

Claire studied knitwear design at college before joining the design team at DMC, and finally going freelance. Claire's work has appeared in several magazines, including *Cross Stitch Magic*. Her designs also feature in six David & Charles books: *Cross Stitch Greetings Cards*, *Cross Stitch Alphabets*, *Cross Stitch Angels*, *Cross Stitch Fairies*, *Magical Cross Stitch* and *Quick to Stitch Cross Stitch Cards* and in her books *Cross Stitch Card Collection* and *Picture Your Pet in Cross Stitch*, also published by David & Charles. Claire lives in Gunnislake, Cornwall.

Jane Lydia Henderson

Having stitched for many years Jane became a professional designer in 2004 and has designed pieces for most of the best-selling British cross stitch magazines. In October 2005, she launched her own company under the brand name Cinnamon Cat Designs, which produces high-quality charts and kits to the retail sector. If you liked Jane's 'animal antics' in this book, then check out her other designs and a list of worldwide stockists on her website www. cinnamoncat.com or by telephoning +44 (0)845 838 6151.

Joanne Sanderson

Joanne started cross stitch designing when a friend asked her to produce a chart. Soon afterwards she won a cross stitch design competition in the *World of Cross Stitching* magazine and has been stitching and designing ever since. Joanne now contributes to many needlecraft magazines and produces designs for DMC kits and publications. Her designs also appeared in *Magical Cross Stitch* and *Quick to Stitch Cross Stitch Cards* for David & Charles. Joanne lives in South Yorkshire with her husband and daughter.

Joan Elliott

Joan's creations have been enchanting cross stitch enthusiasts the world over for years and she is a leading artist for Design Works Crafts Inc. Her debut book for David & Charles, *A Cross Stitcher's Oriental Odyssey* was followed by *Cross Stitch Teddies*, *Cross Stitch Sentiments and Sayings*, *Native American Cross Stitch*, and *Cross Stitch Wit & Wisdom*. Her designs also feature in *Magical Cross Stitch* and *Quick to Stitch Cross Stitch Cards*. Joan divides her time between New York and Vermont.

unique cross-stitch designs by Jane Lydia Henderson

Ursula Michael

For over 20 years Ursula Michael has been delighting cross stitchers with her colourful, whimsical designs, which have appeared in stitching magazines, books, kits and home decorating accessories. Combining her love of nature, needlework and an eye for decorative design, she has taken graphic art training, and needle and thread, down many avenues. Ursula contributed to *Magical Cross Stitch*. She lives in Rhode Island, USA.

Lesley Teare

Lesley trained as a textile designer, with a degree in printed and woven textiles. For some years she has been one of DMC's leading designers and her designs have also featured in many of the cross stitch magazines. Lesley has contributed to numerous books for David & Charles, including *Cross Stitch Greetings Cards*, *Cross Stitch Alphabets*, *Cross Stitch Angels*, *Cross Stitch Fairies*, *Magical Cross Stitch* and *Quick to Stitch Cross Stitch Cards*. She is also the author of *101 Weekend Cross Stitch Gifts*, *Travel The World in Cross Stitch* and *Oriental Cross Stitch*. Lesley lives in Hitcham, Suffolk.

Suppliers

UK

Crafts U Love
tel: 01293 776465
www.craftsulove.co.uk
For a good range of albums and craft supplies

Coats Crafts UK
PO Box 22, Lingfield House, McMullen Road, Darlington, County Durham DL1 1YQ
tel: 01325 394237 (consumer helpline)
www.coatscrafts.co.uk
For Anchor stranded cotton (floss) and other embroidery supplies. Coats also supplies some Charles Craft products and Kreinik metallic threads

The Cotton Patch
1285 Stratford Road, Hall Green, Birmingham B28 9AJ
tel: 0121 702 2840
www.cottonpatch.co.uk
For a wide range of fabrics and needlecraft supplies, including Fast2fuse® double-sided interfacing

Craft Creations Limited
1C Ingersoll House, Delamare Road, Cheshunt, Herts EN8 9HD
tel: 019992 781900
www.craftcreations.com
For greetings card blanks and card-making accessories

DMC Creative World
Pullman Road, Wigston, Leicestershire LE18 2DY
tel: 0116 281 1040 fax: 0116 281 3592
www.dmc/cw.com
For a wide range of embroidery supplies and DMC fabrics and threads

Framecraft Miniatures Ltd
Unit 3, Isis House, Lindon Road, Brownhills, West Midlands WS8 7BW
tel/fax (UK): 01543 360842
tel (international): 44 1543 453154
email: sales@framecraft.com
www.framecraft.com

For Mill Hill beads, buttons, charms, wooden and ceramic trinket pots, notebook covers and many other pre-finished items with cross stitch inserts

Heritage Stitchcraft
Redbrook Lane, Brereton, Rugeley, Staffordshire WS15 1QU
tel: +44 (0) 1889 575256
email: enquiries@heritagestitchcraft.com
www.heritagestitchcraft.com
For Zweigart fabrics and other embroidery supplies

TrimCraft (Nottingham) Ltd
Mancor House, Bolsover Street, Hucknall, Nottinghamshire NG15 7TY,
www.trimcraft.co.uk
For papercraft supplies and nearest stockists of Dovecraft ribbons

Willow Fabrics
95 Town Lane, Mobberley, Knutsford, Cheshire WA16 7HH
tel freephone (UK): 0800 0567811
(elsewhere): +44 (0) 1565 87 2225
www.willowfabrics.com
For embroidery fabrics and Madeira threads

USA

C&T Publishing Inc
1651 Challenge Drive, Concord, CA 94520-5206
tel (US): 800-284-1114
tel (international): 925-677-0377
www.ctpub.com
For Fast2fuse® double-sided interfacing

Charles Craft Inc.
PO Box 1049, Laurenburg, NC 28353
tel: 910 844 3521
email: ccraft@carolina.net
www.charlescraft.com
(Coats Crafts UK supply some Charles Craft products in the UK).
For fabrics for cross stitch and many

useful pre-finished items, including –
Baby Soft™ Afghan fabric, code AF 7311-6750-EA
Bib with pink gingham trim, code BB-3650-5640-EA

Design Works Crafts Inc
170 Wilbur Place
Bohemia, New York 11716
tel: 631 244 5749 fax: 631 244 6138
email: customerservice@designworkscrafts.com
For card mounts and cross stitch kits of Joan Elliott designs

Kreinik Manufacturing Company Inc
3106 Timanus Lane, Suite 101
Baltimore, MD 21244
tel: 1 800 537 2166
email: kreinik@kreinik.com
www.kreinik.com
For a wide range of metallic threads and blending filaments

Thermoweb
www.thermoweb.com
For HeatnBond iron-on adhesive

The WARM Company
954 East Union Street, Seattle, WA 98122
tel: 1 800 234 WARM
www.warmcompany.com
UK Distributor: W. Williams & Sons Ltd
tel: 017 263 7311
For polyester filling, cotton wadding (batting) and Steam-a-Seam fusible web

Zweigart/Joan Toggit Ltd
262 Old Brunswick Road, Suite E, Piscataway, NJ 08854-3756
tel: 732 562 8888
email: info@zweigart.com
www.zweigart.com
For a large selection of cross stitch fabrics and pre-finished table linens

Acknowledgments

The publishers would like to thank the following people for their contributions: Claire Crompton, Joan Elliott, Jane Henderson, Ursula Michael, Joanne Sanderson and Lesley Teare.

Additional thanks to Lin Clements for writing and editing the project and preparing the charts, and to Kim Sayer and Michael Crocker for the photography.

Thanks also to Charles Craft Inc, for the supply of products and fabrics (see Suppliers). Jane Henderson would like to thank her Mum, June Millington, for all her support and the hours she spent stitching Jane's designs. What a star! She would also like to thank Cara Ackerman at DMC Creative World for supplying the threads for her designs in this book.

Index